CW00969588

Challenging Times

stories of Buddhist practice when things get tough

Vishvapani (editor)

windhorse publications

Published by
Windhorse Publications Ltd
11 Park Road
Birmingham
B13 8AB
United Kingdom

Cover image: photograph © Digital Vision
Cover design: Marlene Eltschig
Printed by Cromwell Press Ltd, Trowbridge, England

A catalogue record for this book is available from the British Library
ISBN-10: 1 899579 76 1
ISBN-13: 978 1 899579 76 1

'Raising the Stakes' first appeared in *Tricycle: The Buddhist Review*, no.58.

Contents

acknowledgements

This book is a by-product of *Dharma Life* magazine, which was a labour of love for many people over nine years. A number of the articles were produced in the 'People' section of the magazine and hunted out by its three editors: Vidyadevi, Subhadramati, and Vajrasara. All three share a feeling for Dharma practice and an interest in people that helped them to find many of these writers and draw out their stories, and it was a pleasure to work with all of them. The idea for this book came from Subhadramati, which showed again her belief in the power of these stories.

Time and again I was amazed by the writers' willingness to be so open about their experience and their struggles, and to share them so eloquently. That contribution lies at the heart of this book.

Nagabodhi, Kulananda, Kulamitra, and Dhammarati all offered editorial support and gave feedback on the articles. And Guhyapati, Jyotika, Vandanajyoti, and Theresa del Soldato contributed through their involvement in the *Dharma Life* team. The magazine was generously supported by the European Chairs meeting of the Friends of the Western Buddhist Order, and Sangharakshita and Subhuti gave much encouragement to me and the others in the team over the years.

The staff of Windhorse Publications worked faithfully in the background to support *Dharma Life*, often with little acknowledgement and certainly with little income; and now they have done the same again with *Challenging Times*. Thanks to Jnanasiddhi for her editorial input, and to everyone else at Windhorse for their dedication and hard work.

The inferno of the living is not something that will be; if there is one, it is what is already here, the inferno where we live every day, that we form by being together. There are two ways to escape suffering it. The first is easy for many: accept the inferno and become such a part of it that you can no longer see it. The second is risky and demands constant vigilance and apprehension: seek and learn to recognize who and what, in the midst of the inferno, are not inferno, then make them endure, give them space.

Italo Calvino, *Invisible Cities*

introduction

Vishvapani

One day, in the middle of a busy magazine production period, a tiny Tibetan monk with shrivelled skin and sunken eyes came to visit me in my London office. His name was Palden Gyatso and he was in London to discuss his book, *Fire Under the Snow*, about his experiences as a political prisoner in Tibet. It describes the torture he went through, the friends and teachers who were killed, and the tragedy of the Tibetan experience after the Chinese invasion. But the most remarkable aspect of the book is Palden's response. I wanted to ask him whether it was really true, as he claimed, that he did not hate the Chinese, even the guards who tortured him. Or was that more of an aspiration.

Palden spoke quietly and through a translator, but he looked at me intently with sad, thoughtful eyes as he tried to put his experience into words. 'It is not that I was without hatred. Especially when I was being tortured by my guards I had immense hatred against them, because I was being hurt. But as a religious person, after the event I could reflect on what had happened and I could see that the torturers were acting out of their own ignorance. As a religious person I have to sit back, reflect, and ask myself, what is all this? Our teaching says, "Don't let your calm be disturbed and don't respond to anger with anger."'

I published an account of the meeting in *Dharma Life* magazine, which I edited for nine years, and on the cover of the issue in which it appeared we printed a photo of Palden's ravaged face covered over by his hands, breaking into tears as he recalled his experiences. It was a strong image, but I regretted a little that it did not show his face. My abiding memory of Palden is of the thick, leathery feel of those hands when he gripped mine as he said goodbye, and the intense, focused energy of his smile. His words had been so simple and so direct that I had no doubts about his sincerity. I sensed that, rather than being over-whelmed by his sufferings, he had faced them directly, until eventually he became greater than them. Returning to my desk, tape recorder in hand, I felt blessed.

During the years I was editing *Dharma Life*, every so often, amid the scurrying for deadlines and searching for writers, a contribu-tion would arrive that conveyed such depth, such honesty, and often such eloquence that it stopped me short. These had often been commissioned by one of my fellow editors. At other times I met and interviewed extraordinary men and women like Palden Gyatso, whose stories reminded me why I was interested in producing a Buddhist magazine. They weren't just *about* the practice of Buddhism – they embodied it.

Many of the most powerful articles were about the experience of men and women who had been faced with difficulties. Some-times these difficulties went far beyond my own mild struggles: a life-threatening illness, addiction, chronic pain, or, in the most dramatic stories, the murder of a relative or life on Death Row. Sometimes they were the more ordinary struggles of daily life. In each case the writer had reached a point where their usual ways of coping no longer worked and they were forced to ask, 'What can I do now that I have a difficulty that can't be fixed by continuing to act as I usually do, and I am suffering?'. These writers had turned to Buddhist practice for a way out, but the challenges they faced were universal human experiences.

A year after Palden Gyatso's visit I made a journey of my own. I had no experiences in my own life to compare even remotely with what he had been through, but my father had fled to Eng-land as a refugee from the Nazis, and his own father had been killed in a concentration camp. I decided to attend a 'Bearing Witness' retreat at Auschwitz, and found myself sitting by the Berkenau railway tracks, in the bitter November cold, surrounded by other retreatants. I took a moment to consider what I was experiencing, and to my shock I realized I was feeling blank and neutral. I had expected to feel something extraordinary that did justice to the darkness of what had happened. Instead, I found that it was just me, with all my habits, distractions, and fantasies, relocated to a place where others had been through extraordinary suffering. I grew anxious: was I emotionally lacking, or superficial, or unaware? Why wasn't I feeling what I should be feeling?

As I relate in my account of that retreat, which is included in this book, my experience did change over the few days I was at Berkenau, but I learned as much from that feeling of blankness and the anxiety it provoked as I did from any of the stronger feelings that arose later on. I realized that I had to stop trying to make my experience fit what I thought it ought to be, and be true to what it actually was. I needed to pay attention, to wait, to be mindful, and to be open to what was happening. Being at Auschwitz was so distressing that it took some time to open myself to it, even a little. What struck me most about this experience was that it seemed so familiar. It was the same feeling that I had when I was irritated with a friend or a train was delayed. Being in a concentration camp dramatized the process, but essentially it was no different from the choice I faced every day: to turn towards my experience and other people, or to turn away.

Reading through these articles again, what strikes me most is that the encounter with suffering is not necessarily exciting or dramatic, even though some of the writers are describing quite extreme and unusual experiences. The Hollywood version of suffering is that it is a cue for struggle and redemption, triumph through adversity. But what was so impressive about these stories of Buddhist experiences of working with difficulties is that the writers were not trying to escape from or transcend any-

3

thing. They often recognized that much of their previous way of living had already been an attempt to escape feelings of disease and anxiety, but their writing describes their decision, now that the old strategy wasn't working any more, to turn to face themselves and their defences with courage and honesty.

I won't say much about the Buddhist background to these accounts: a lot of that is described by the various writers as they tell their stories. But it is worth saying that answering the question, 'What can I do now that I have a difficulty that can't be fixed by continuing to act as I usually have, and I am suffering?' is the whole point of Buddhist practice. This is pretty much what the Buddha had in mind when he identified *duḥkha* as the first of his Four Noble Truths. *Duḥkha* means 'suffering', but it also suggests unsatisfactoriness, dis-ease, lack, and incompleteness. The Buddha's second Truth identifies the cause of the problem as the tendency to want things to be different; as he said, 'the origin of *duḥkha* is craving'. This craving is the desire to be somewhere else, doing something else. The alternative is being *here*, doing *this*, even if it is painful.

The practice of facing up to experience is what powers these articles. They describe what can happen when we stop complaining about our distress or distracting ourselves from it and face it directly. What can happen, it turns out, includes the joy, forgiveness, generosity, contentment, courage, and determination that also fills these pages. These stories brim with the discovery of a sense of purpose and greater connection with other people, and that, too, is part of Buddhist practice.

Since *Dharma Life* ceased publication in 2005, the articles collected in *Challenging Times* have stood out in my mind as having enduring worth. I love them for their honesty and openheartedness, for their sincerity and courage, and they deserve to continue to be read and pondered. The magazine explored the encounter of Buddhism and the modern world, and over the years various writers have suggested where the true cutting edge of that encounter is taking place: in the translation of texts, in the practice of social engagement, in the practice of psychotherapy and cross-cultural discussions of the mind, or in this or that Buddhist movement. All those things are laudable, but for me, the surest sign that Buddhism is truly connecting with Western culture is found in stories such as these, which show Western people applying the teachings to their lives in down-to-earth and effective ways. Their stories aren't really about Buddhism at all – East or West, past or present. They are about our most ordinary habits and responses, including our most personal feelings of aloneness and anxiety, and how these feelings conceal the hidden magnitudes of the truth of our lives.

Some of these ordinary Buddhists are famous teachers, and some of the others have exotic-sounding Indian names. This is because they are members of the Western Buddhist Order and were given those names at ordination. *Dharma Life* was produced by the Friends of the Western Buddhist Order, and the FWBO and its founder, Sangharakshita, get quite a few mentions in the text. I think that being embedded in a particular community of practitioners helped keep the magazine grounded, and connected with individuals' daily practice. Such a community also offers a context for people to share their practice honestly and openly, and perhaps that helped as well.

These stories make up the *Voices* of Part One of this book. I have arranged them by theme: working with the mind in difficult circumstances; practising in prison, confronting illness, facing death, and some other personal stories. Part Two includes *Reflections* from four well-known teachers on suffering and how to respond to it, as well as other discussions of the path beyond anger towards compassion.

Compassion is what happens when kindness meets pain. The reason I love these articles is that so much compassion shines through them. It is born of courage, as real as a rock and with the wisdom of experience deeply lived.

PART ONE:*voices*

forgiving my sister's killers

Marian Partington
interviewed by Vajrasara

One night in 1973 my sister vanished. Our family then endured two decades of not knowing what had happened to Lucy. The anguish of uncertainty seemed, if anything, to increase over the years. By 1994 I had become desperate – my biggest fear was that we'd die without ever discovering. And my distress grew more acute as my eldest son approached 21 (Lucy's age when she disappeared). But 1994 was to be a momentous year for me.

Back in 1973 we were at home in the English Cotswolds for the Christmas holidays. Lucy was 21 and I was 26, two of four siblings. We were both studying English at university. She was single-minded and passionately exploring the deeper meaning of life. I was more hedonistic, into flower-power and living with my boyfriend. Yet we shared a love of literature, particularly T.S. Eliot's *Four Quartets*, and his concept of 'the still point of the turning world'. On 27 December Lucy went to visit a friend in Cheltenham. She was due to catch the last bus home, but she never caught that bus. Her disappearance led to a national search, and an inquiry room operated for seven years, but to no avail. For over twenty years this remained an unresolved part of our lives.

It was an agonizing period for our family. It was hard to stay present to the huge loss, and talking about Lucy became almost taboo. Yet because we didn't talk about her it was like she'd never existed. We'd had no funeral or any formal gathering to mark her life, but it seemed as if we were privately acknowledging she was

9

dead. I have learned a lot about the complexity of unresolved grief.

Somehow my life continued and I finished my degree. My pain and lack of spiritual direction led to destructive choices at first, but I gave birth to three lovely children, settled with my partner, and eventually trained as a homoeopath. However, Lucy's continued absence was a reality I couldn't avoid. Whenever anyone went out of the door there was the prospect I might never see them again. That anxiety affected my confidence in dealing with life and undermined my ability to trust myself and others. The 'not knowing' led to a frozen silence, part of me was still hoping … stuck in the past.

One positive consequence was that Lucy's disappearance intensified my awareness of the present. I really appreciated being alive. Looking back, now through Buddhist eyes, it was a strong teaching. It meant I could never feel complacent about life. I also knew it was a challenge and I needed to find an inner way of working with it.

Becoming a homoeopath inspired a quest to understand and work with the process of healing. I learned to listen to others' suffering and prescribe remedies to help them find a healthy relationship with their pain. Doing this as an unprejudiced observer became an important part of my own journey. I realized that becoming whole involves integrating the pain of the past. So, by 1994, after over twenty years, everything was in place to 'rediscover' Lucy. I was in a stable relationship, my children were growing up, and I had fifteen years' experience in helping others to heal.

By February 1994, a horrific news story was emerging in Gloucester about the serial killers Fred and Rosemary West, and I had a hunch that it was connected with Lucy. On 4 March – Lucy's birthday – Fred West told the police there were more bodies buried in the basement of 25 Cromwell Street, and that one of them was Lucy's. Dental records later confirmed it was indeed her.

She was one of twelve young women who had been tortured, raped, and murdered. I shudder at her unimaginable physical and emotional suffering. The Wests beheaded and dismembered Lucy, and stuffed her into a small hole surrounded by leaking sewage pipes. The notorious West case became known in Britain as the crime of the century; they had pushed sadomasochism to its limit and needed an influx of live human victims to feed their habit.

The shock of Lucy's bones being unearthed had the impact, for me, of a Zen insight: everything I'd once known was stripped of meaning. What was I left with? In the following weeks I felt terribly vulnerable, but this experience was a reality I wanted to understand, because it felt true. I was left with the raw truth.

We weren't yet allowed to have Lucy's bones back, so we could not have a funeral. They were kept as 'exhibits for the defence' for another year. But I was keen to see what was left of my sister, so in May I contacted the police and went with two friends to the mortuary to perform a ceremony. There was nothing fearful or morbid about it – I was full of joy at finding something of Lucy after all these years.

I wanted to wrap her bones and treat what was left of her with love and tenderness, to reclaim her from her murderers and that hugely disrespectful, wretched hole in their cellar. I decided to place special items in the coffin, and something to represent the elements: a sprig of heather (earth), rescue remedy (water), a candle (fire), and some incense (air).

I gasped at the sight of her skull – it was so beautiful, like burnished gold. Holding her skull was very intense: for a moment I 'knew' a deep reality, and felt that what I was doing was not just for Lucy but for everyone who had suffered a violent death. I

11

wrapped Lucy's skull in her soft brown blanket, while her friend placed some cherished childhood possessions inside to guard her bones. We lit a candle and held hands in silence; somehow we seemed united again within 'the still point of the turning world'. I felt in contact with something ancestral and timeless.

Our family was not religious, but shortly before Lucy was murdered she had been received into the Roman Catholic Church. I was also interested in spiritual matters, and Buddhism had been on the margins of my life for years. However, I came to Buddhism via Quakerism. When my daughter was nine she asked to be christened and I wanted to support her, but I felt uneasy about God. Then I remembered Quakers and their silent form of worship, which seemed sufficiently open, so I began going to meetings in 1987. It became increasingly meaningful to explore this spiritual path alongside other seekers.

Just a week after our ceremony with the bones, my partner and I went on a Western Zen retreat. It felt timely – I had so much to assimilate – and uncannily appropriate. I was astonished when the retreat leader, Dr John Crook, used a hollowed human thigh bone as a musical instrument: after my recent experience with Lucy's bones, it was almost unbelievable. I discovered that this ceremonial instrument, from Tibetan Buddhist culture, is traditionally made from the thigh bone of a criminal, and that blowing through it was thought ritually to purify their karma. This coincidence and other resonances convinced me that exploring Buddhism was my next step.

John Crook suggested that the more I could share of my suffering, the more it would help others. It became clear that meditation would be immensely valuable. I saw how Buddhism offered the tools to face the reality of human violence – as well as my own potential for that. And it gave me the means to work towards inner resolution without being crippled by negative emotions. So 1994 was also the year I started to practise the Dharma.

A year later I went on my second Buddhist retreat with Ch'an Master Sheng Yen. In the interim Fred West had killed himself, Lucy's bones had been released, and we finally had a proper funeral. The week beforehand I had attended Rosemary West's committal trial. I wanted to know as much as I could about what had happened before it hit the media. But listening to the evidence, the stream of brutality and crude sexual detail, I felt I was being corrupted. I became aware of the huge need for purification. I knew I had to make this journey towards peace without denying human atrocity.

Before that retreat, I realized that what I needed to learn from Master Sheng Yen was humility and gratitude. I was conscious of a lot of pride and ingratitude within. And this is exactly what he chose to teach. We did lots of meditation and prostrations. At the end of the retreat I made a vow aloud: I would work towards forgiving.

When I got home, the first thing I experienced was murderous rage. The previous year my energies had centred on laying Lucy to rest. But now, having had the funeral and heard those ghastly details, tremendous rage erupted. It was a pure rage, intense and very physical: a great heat kept rising up from my belly and exploding inside my skull. It was terribly frightening. I realized I was capable of killing, and that I couldn't ever dismiss people who had acted out of a fury like this. So my path towards forgiving began with murderous rage.

During Rosemary West's trial, I was anxious to protect children from learning about their depravities through the media, so I imagined creating a national diversion by hanging poems in trees in memory of all victims of violence. The idea stemmed from one of Lucy's favourite poems by Yevtushenko: 'I hung a poem on a branch'.

I didn't have the energy to pursue the idea, but I was excited at this time to discover Tibetan prayer flags, which symbolize compassion and interconnectedness. A colourful row of them now traces the wind outside my kitchen window.

I already knew all the details, but I went to the judge's summing up. Hearing that Rosemary would be locked away for life gave me no satisfaction. I was not interested in vengeance. I was most disturbed by the fact that Lucy had been gagged, and couldn't speak her truth. I'd had a sore throat for the whole six weeks of the trial. I knew from my experience as a homeopath that I needed to speak, to communicate what I knew of Lucy's story.

So I contacted the *Guardian* newspaper and they suggested I wrote about it. Using meditation, I sat with whatever arose, then tried to find words for it. It took five months and was deeply healing. The very long article drew a huge response – over 300 letters and poems – and I was awarded a grant from a charitable trust to continue my inner journey, meditation retreats, and writing. I knew I had work to do on forgiving. I needed a support group and I found this in the Western Ch'an Fellowship, and the Quaker community.

The next year was dominated by grief. After twenty years of not knowing, the horrific discovery, the media onslaught, the trials, and the rage, finally came the grief. It first arose on another retreat with John Crook. I knew I had to confront this torrent of grief: the emphasis of Ch'an is all about self-confrontation. But I was concerned I might make a noise – and we were on a silent retreat.

However, I trusted John Crook; his response to my story of wrapping Lucy's bones had been so positive. Previously I had only grieved in private but now I turned towards it in meditation and tears flooded out. I could see why life is known as a 'vale of tears'. Endless tears and snot – I just observed, without wiping them away. I wanted it to be as it was – the truth of a very sad experience.

In one meditation I was feeling self-pity, wading alone in this lake of tears, when suddenly the lake was filled with everyone who'd experienced bereavement by murder – people from the Holocaust, from Rwanda, from all the wars and atrocities of the world. Once I had made that connection, the pain subsided. As the retreat progressed I just sat. I felt so present and at ease, I didn't move for three periods of meditation. I reached the bottom of my grief: a genuine purification of emotion. Previously I tried to protect others (especially my children) from my grief, but since then I haven't hidden it.

On my last retreat with Master Sheng Yen, I became aware that acute pain was starting to erupt – yet again. I was having great trouble drawing breath. I realized I didn't want to go on breathing. It gave me an insight into why people killed themselves – why they didn't want to go on breathing. It was as if I was turning all that negative emotion inward, and I didn't want to carry on living.

I reflected on what we do with our unresolved pain. Not expressing the pain can lead to suicide. Acting it out leads to violence and brutality. Wishing it away, repression, or denial leads to physical illness. The only creative way forward with so much pain is to inch towards forgiving.

In a meditation interview I said despairingly that I was dealing with a huge karmic obstruction. I asked Master Sheng Yen whether I had become too attached to this overwhelming aspect of my life. He replied, 'No, it's real, you must be true to it. But remember that your suffering will help to relieve the suffering of others.'

'Yes. But what's the practice? *Tonglen* meditation (breathing in others' suffering and breathing out compassion), prayer, or what?'

After returning to my cushion, I had a startling insight into Rose-mary West's great suffering: locked away for life, isolated, demonized, estranged from her children.… As if for the first time I empathized deeply with her tragic position. I found myself praying that my pain would relieve hers. All my suffering dissolved. I had lived with this burning question of how to feel compassion for someone who had 'ruined my life' – and in that moment I knew. I experienced a spacious open heart, where for-giving is spontaneous.

I prefer to think in terms of 'forgiving', which suggests an on-going process; the noun 'forgiveness' suggests something more final. Practising Buddhism helps to align me ethically so that I can develop a forgiving attitude. It reminds me that I'm doing this not just for myself but for my parents, my children, for the next generation – and also for Rosemary West. Every day, one of the Buddhist vows that I recite is, 'I vow to deliver innumerable sentient beings from suffering.'

A woman whose daughter was murdered told me that 'forgive-ness means giving up all hope of a better past'. To do this I have to face my own past, my mistakes, and find out how to purify and integrate them, accepting the reality of what happened to my sister – and not being distracted by what we'll never know. It is a big discipline and I couldn't do it without the Buddha's teachings, the spiritual community, and periods of solitude.

A couple of years ago I was invited to the International Confer-ence on Restorative Justice. I was inspired by what I heard. I was already convinced that the labels 'victim' and 'offender' were inadequate. I had come to realize that these people – supposedly so different – have the same needs. Both need a safe place to explore their pain and accept the truth of what has happened. Restorative justice seems to soften that sharp separation and opposition.

It is the only method I've come across that offers a positive way forward. Crime is viewed as harm done that needs healing, which often involves mediation between victims and offenders. Restorative justice is a voluntary process in which both sides listen to each other; it can lead naturally to reconciliation and even forgiveness. If both people can talk about their lives, the perpetrator usually expresses remorse. Consequently the victim feels more generous towards them. This tends to bring deeper understanding – seeing the other person as a suffering human being.

Without such a meeting, the victim is often left with unresolved pain, which may well harden into vengeful prejudice, while the perpetrator might understand the consequences of their action. They also might not. Results vary, but it is such a worthwhile endeavour.

I've been drawn to work in restorative justice through glimpses of my own Buddha-nature. In Bristol Prison I became involved in a project to raise victim awareness with staff, and among some prisoners. Usually, I explain my story, including my experiences of extremely destructive emotion. Then I listen to their stories, trying to help them open their hearts to themselves.

There was a young man in prison for burglary who was very moved by my story and my likening what happened to Lucy to the ultimate burglary. He suddenly saw that his crimes had affected others' lives. So he asked to be taken back to his flat where he showed police all the other items he'd stolen; he was driven around pointing out the houses he had burgled and asked the police to return the goods and express his apologies. He didn't expect it to have much effect but it made a huge difference to him, because he suddenly realized he had more choice.

He and I are corresponding – he has written beautiful poems about forgiveness, truth, and the seeds of hope. It was clearly a significant insight, which probably changed his life. When he left prison I helped him get into a residential situation where he would have one-to-one help. I know he's still struggling, but he hasn't returned to drugs or crime. This relationship satisfies me deeply.

I have also been to Grendon Prison. Their therapeutic approach involves holding visitors' days. In our group there were six visitors and six prisoners – each spoke about why they were there. I said I was motivated to understand how these extreme feelings that I, too, had experienced came to be acted out in violence. I said the fact that Lucy had been gagged meant she couldn't speak her truth, and I was interested in listening to their truth.

One of the prisoners who had committed multiple rape then looked me in the eye and said, 'Something you said has just hit home. Until you spoke I was just playing at victim empathy.' It clearly helped him to understand what he'd done. I don't know what has happened to him but again it meant a lot to me.

I recently returned to Bristol Prison and spent time listening to prisoners serving life sentences. I would love them to learn meditation – they have so much spare time. I'm not ready to teach it myself, but hopefully I can support that happening. I am moved by the acute loneliness of people who have made grave mistakes and been written off by friends and family. I feel drawn to help. So often they have nobody to talk to – prison seldom encourages meaningful communication. There are a few religious ministers who visit prisons; perhaps that's the way my work will lead. I seem to be in an unusual position, in that I can help prisoners to open their hearts by sharing my perspective.

Ideally, I would like to have a meeting with Rosemary West, but since she has denied anything to do with Lucy's death, she's unlikely to agree to meet me. Those who know her have advised me that it is not yet time to suggest it. I am planning to send her a letter, though. Meanwhile I am content to continue sending her compassion. It is almost ten years since the discovery and I've noticed that other cases of victim–perpetrator mediation often occur after ten to fifteen years. So maybe the time is ripening....

I recently went on my first solitary retreat and practised the visualization meditation of Green Tāra. She is described as the quintessence of compassion, and I know compassion and the understanding that we are all connected are the keys to encouraging forgiveness. And over the years I have responded strongly to Kṣitigarbha, the bodhisattva who watches over the hell realms and brings help to all beings in misery and torment.

I also came across this verse by the Dalai Lama, which struck my heart.

> I will learn to cherish beings of bad nature
> And those pressed by strong sins and suffering
> As if I had found a precious
> Treasure very difficult to find.

What an inspiration, and an awesome challenge. I know Lucy would have understood the meaning of the words 'love thy neighbour'. This path of forgiving offers a way to break the cycle of violence and hatred, to reach towards the experience of profound compassion and humility. Lucy's life and death have deepened my knowledge of love. I dearly hope to pass that on.

_confronting myself

Subhadramati

Seeing a map of all the FWBO Buddhist centres that had no women teachers was what clinched my decision to move to Dublin. Although women became involved with Buddhist practice, they lacked the inspiration and friendship of more experienced women. A friend of mine was planning to move to Dublin and I decided to join her. But it wasn't an easy decision; I was leaving a mature spiritual community, where I had many good friends, for a situation in which I would have to be more self-reliant. I was frightened, but I knew I couldn't live with myself if I let fear stop me.

There are two main aspects to my work in Dublin: the Evolution gift shop run by a team of Buddhist women, and the Dublin Meditation Centre itself. My experience of teaching at a Buddhist centre was limited. At the centre I had been involved with there were plenty of people who could give talks and lead festivals, so I only had an occasional opportunity. But there were just four of us in Dublin. Believing it was important that a woman should be giving talks at the Dublin Centre, I threw myself into its work.

That first year was fantastic. I experienced my own effectiveness, though most of what I contributed was sharing what I had learned in London. Probably I was over-excited; whenever I sat to meditate my head was buzzing with ideas about what I could do next. I felt engaged and fulfilled and didn't want to be doing anything else. I remember thinking, 'I'll work as hard as I can and don't care if it kills me, it'll be worth it.'

Working in the shop was much more familiar as I had spent ten years in another Buddhist-run business, a restaurant. I believe strongly in the effectiveness of what we call 'team-based right livelihood' as a means of developing oneself spiritually. I even think that working in a team that has an emphasis on Buddhist practice can be a more effective means of change than going on retreat. To an outsider it might seem like merely shop work, but our approach makes a Buddhist shop quite different.

You are faced with yourself – your own tendencies – every day. There is no escape. In working together on a common project there will inevitably be differing opinions about the best way to operate. No one is the boss, so to reach agreement you have to negotiate. You need to communicate and come to an understanding. All the time you are trying to practise Buddhist ethics and helping others to do so. It can be like heaven and it can be hell. If you are engaged it is effective, but when you aren't it is tremendously challenging.

Although I believed in this work, I had a difficulty. Previously I'd worked with people with whom I had built up a connection over the years. I could share what I was working on in my spiritual life, and they could help me. Now I was with people for whom all this was new, it was an experiment rather than a commitment. There was a high turnover of staff, many working part-time or for only a few months. I didn't feel able to share myself in the way I used to.

Initially I felt frustrated. Then I came up with a different approach. I saw myself as leading a series of retreats. It was obvious that most of the people working in the shop were benefiting. I saw how they gained confidence and clarity about their lives, even if they didn't stay. The benefit for me was that I was helping them. Nothing had changed externally but I felt more content.

However, it didn't challenge me. I was coasting along, more engrossed by activities at the Centre. By this time, as well as teaching, I was increasingly involved with hammering out the principles of how to run things. I had to think more clearly and be more outspoken than ever before. As these new qualities were being drawn out of me, I felt the Centre was my real practice ground.

But a year after my arrival in Dublin a crunch came in the shop. Christmas was by far our busiest time and it had gone well. Three experienced women had come from the UK for three months to help out. We had made lots of money to give to our centre and other Buddhist projects. But on Christmas Eve it dawned on me that the extra helpers would be going, leaving a team of three full-timers instead of the six we needed. And the others were planning to be away over and above their usual retreat time.

I was catapulted into disillusionment. I started to ask, 'What am I doing here? I want to give an opportunity to others, but if no one wants to take this opportunity what's the point?' I had a koan, a deeply-felt spiritual conundrum: if my practice is to be a spiritual friend yet there is no one to befriend, then how can I practise? I felt this koan was tearing me apart. And yet, I reflected, if I am truly practising, my well-being shouldn't be dependent on what other people do. Why, then, am I so unhappy?

I felt lonely because I couldn't share my ideals. I started to fantasize about leaving Dublin and going somewhere with lots of other members of the Western Buddhist Order. Meanwhile, I was frustrated and resentful towards those who weren't working in the shop and those who wanted to take time out. I wanted to take hold of them, turn their heads around, and make them look at the opportunity they were missing.

I had a feeling that I was looking at the situation wrongly. I needed a key to open some lock in my mind. I was fed up with

23

talking about practical solutions. I knew that whatever was making me unhappy lay within. I wanted to feel potent again, but I didn't know how. I knew I had something to offer and I suffered the frustration of being unable to give it. Eventually I went back to the UK to talk things through with various long-standing friends. I mentioned to one the irritation I often felt with others on the team, and she burst out, 'You are talking about being irritated as if that was just incidental or insignificant. Don't you see: *that* is the core problem you have to work on!' For a few seconds I was shocked by her directness. Then I felt tremendously excited. This was my key, something concrete I could engage with. I needed to work on my tendency to get irritated. And I wanted to start right away!

Actually I have tried to work on my irritability for years. I experience it in situations where I care about what is happening, and I think it is the flip side of being engaged. Over the years I have become more successful at not letting it out. I try not to be horrible to people – and if I am I make sure I apologize. But when my friend asked me if that had worked, I had to admit that, no, in all the years of trying to contain my annoyance I didn't think it had changed or lessened. It was still the same inside.

Putting this in traditional Buddhist terms, I had just been trying to purify my actions of body and speech. But Buddhism teaches that one must work directly on the mind. That is the only solution. My excitement came from seeing how I could change something that seemed a part of me. I reflected on the familiar advice: 'If you want to change the world you have to change yourself,' and I felt its truth. I had lofty aims like 'I want to communicate my vision', 'I want to be a spiritual friend'; but I saw that it boils down to whether I can get on with the person I'm working with. 'How unglamorous,' I thought, 'it hardly sounds exciting, but actually it is the key.'

Since then, I have recommitted myself to working in a team as a means of transforming myself. Giving public talks and leading courses are tasks I have to work hard at, but they are less demanding than working in the shop. People quite often tell me that I'm great, or inspiring. And I feel great, I feel inspiring. But it's easier to do those things than to communicate with someone who hasn't done what they were meant to do – without being harsh. It is simple compared with being friendly when somebody interrupts me in the middle of something I think is important, or when I just don't feel very kind. These daily interactions are where the work lies. When I find my closest work partner is someone I don't understand and who doesn't understand me, the hard thing is to share myself with them, especially when I think they won't understand me. It's less visible, and no one will be saying, 'You're so inspiring.' But this is what will change me.

So what do I actually do? When I'm irritated I ask myself what is going on. I have identified several types of irritation. Sometimes I get irritated with people, sometimes with things. Often I move quickly from inspiration to over-excitement to irritation. Most often I get irritated by running imaginary scenarios in my head in which people aren't doing their jobs properly. It's a type of righteous indignation.

I have started to do the *karuṇā bhāvanā* (development of compassion) meditation practice several times a week. This involves contemplating the suffering of others: friends, those I barely know, enemies. It doesn't come naturally to me. I tend to empathize more with people's joys and successes than with their struggles. I reflected that one of the ten ethical precepts that I undertake as a member of the Western Buddhist Order is changing hatred into compassion (rather than simply love) – and irritation is a form of hatred. During the day, if I find I am irritated I reflect on compassion – for example, that the person who was rude to me was feeling insecure. This quickly transforms it.

I asked a more experienced practitioner how he had worked with irritation. His reply was uncompromising: 'I reflect that it is a thoroughly immature and selfish emotion.' Again, for a moment, I felt shock and then tremendous excitement. I thought, 'This practice can radically change the way I relate to the world. It's so easy to feel justified in my irritation – I feel I'm standing up for principles, in my view I'm a heroine! But the reason I become irritated is that I want things my own way and under my control. There's no doubt about it. It's not about what's going on out there, it's about what's happening in my mind. If I can see this I feel so ashamed and embarrassed that the irritation fades.

I now find that asking myself the simple question, 'Who is it that's getting irritated?' is usually enough to help me see through it. In these ways I am learning how to deal with my irritability directly: to see my mental tendency, and to change it. This has an entirely different flavour from simply not expressing the negativity.

Recently someone overlooked something I thought was important. This is the kind of incident that usually provokes me into righteous annoyance. But this time I genuinely felt sympathy. I thought how hard they had been working and how difficult it is to remember everything. I was delighted and a little amazed. What I had been practising was actually working!

I am starting to have a sense of what replaces irritation: the feeling of being connected. Being irritable gives me the illusion that I'm upholding standards; I feel important. But the sense of connection is far more rewarding.

I now see that the most valuable part of my time in Dublin has been the difficulties. I reached my limits and I didn't know what to do, but it became clear that I could not carry on in the same way. It's easy to become comfortable in circumstances that don't confront one's habits, and difficult to see it from within. Had I not put myself in challenging conditions by leaving the large, supportive situation in London, I would probably not have made this breakthrough. I would have had ups and downs, I would have argued with people and had to make up. But less challenging circumstances might not have brought me up against myself so starkly. Being here I have felt more visible, so the consequences of my actions seem more significant. It was imperative that I change for the better. I have been forced me to go deeper – and I think I personally needed to be forced.

When you reach that crisis point you need friendship and support, otherwise the difficulties will probably overwhelm you. I don't know how I would have managed if I hadn't had good, long-standing friends to call on at any time. If I'd given up I expect everyone would have been sympathetic. They would probably have said that things were just too difficult. But I knew that if I had given up it would have been because I didn't have sufficient spiritual resources. I have been focusing on meditation and ethical practice to build up a reservoir of inner strength.

It might seem surprising that discovering my limits has been a source of happiness, but the happiness comes from being engaged with the truth – not the story my ego is weaving. I certainly haven't mastered my tendency to irritability, but I have found a creative way to work with it. And this is just one area of practice, just one part of myself that has to change. I hope there will be many more insights to come.

I wasn't ready to come to Dublin. I discovered that I needed more qualities than I had so far developed. But as Sanghapala, the man who pioneered FWBO activities in Dublin, told me, 'If you wait until you are ready you will never become ready.' You just have to act; you will come up against your limits, and new qualities will emerge.

_healing the scars of abuse

'Sarah'

'It's Sarah. I love you. I ask you to forgive me.' I whispered to the motionless old woman, lying in her hospital bed. I leaned over and kissed her, and a shudder went through her whole body. Then I sang Milarepa's 'Song of Meeting and Parting'. The next day the hospital telephoned to say she had died in the night. I had visited just in time.

The old woman was my grandmother. The moment I said the words 'forgive me', I felt everything that had ever troubled me about our relationship was resolved. It was as if the word itself had ritual power. Faced with her death, I had realized what was most important.

Six years previously, three years after I'd become a Buddhist, I had been sitting in my flat having just given up an almost life-long habit of smoking cigarettes. I was replaying a recurrent memory, a television programme I had seen as a child showing a man sexually abusing a young girl. With an overwhelming dread I realized that no such thing would ever be broadcast. I rang a Buddhist I knew who was also a psychotherapist and he recommended me to a female therapist, who gave me exercises from a workbook to do.

A few nights later I woke up with a series of memories. The first was my grandmother showing me a newspaper picture of the Prime Minister bending down to speak to a young girl. At the same time she was violently manipulating my genitals. 'This is what he'd really like to be doing,' she said, 'This is what men are like.' The second was of being held up high and dropped onto the bed. It wasn't a fun game, I knew she wanted to frighten me, to give me a sense of her power. Another particularly distressing memory was of being in a disturbing physical condition, like being drugged or drunk. And the one I hated most was of her holding me down on the bed with my knees against my chest. I was saying I wanted to go to the toilet but she wouldn't let me. Looking back I find this particularly sadistic.

Of course, when my parents had come to fetch me from my grandmother's, she was totally different. Then it was all sweeties and cuddles. When you see this you just know other adults would not believe the person to be capable of such things. You begin to doubt yourself. A voice in your head whispers, 'You're lying.' This is how we forget. For me it is the fear of not being believed, or actually not being believed, that causes the most pain. In talking about my experience this was far worse than reliving the actual events.

When, as an adult, I told my mother about these memories she said that after one particular extended visit to my grandmother I came back changed. I walked with my head hanging down and had nightmares in which I talked about photographs. I was two-and-a-half years old. I remember at that time I was really scared of a particular tree in our back garden. It had died of a disease so it had no leaves, only spiky branches sticking starkly out. I hated when the curtains were opened and I had to look at it, and I would never play in the back garden. Looking back, I see this tree as an image of my damaged trust.

The period of time after having these memories was very difficult. I did regress to childhood behaviour: I was crying to go home and crying for my mummy. I remember one particularly horrible experience of going into a café and it resembling a vision by the artist Hogarth. Every time someone moved an arm or a leg it seemed to me sexual. The whole world had become sexual.

I put a lot of trust in my therapist and in the literature she gave me to read. I knew I was in pain and I wanted to be healed. The therapy made a strong link between anger and healing. I was encouraged to recover my anger and I tried my best to be a good client, beating the cushions or whatever. I am not saying that I wasn't angry. I felt a boiling rage that I could not enjoy my sexuality. Until this point I thought I was a sexual pervert – that was even how I introduced myself to my therapist. I thought I had been born that way, just as some people are born physically handicapped.

Sexual encounters made me freeze up. The first time I spent the night with a boyfriend I ended up sleeping in the bath. Then I discovered I could go through with sex if I withdrew into my own world of fantasy, but this made me feel ashamed and abnormal. Until I went to therapy I felt depressed, and resigned to the fact I could never be normal. Therapy helped with this. My therapist would repeat to me that I was not abnormal, that she (my grandmother) had done this to me.

However, I think, especially where relatives are involved, we can feel a mixture of emotions, sometimes anger and sometimes love. If we focus on anger and vengeance as the only way of healing, then we leave out love and forgiveness. But the literature I came across suggested that forgiveness was a weakness or, worse, could militate against the healing process. In one book there was a whole chapter on challenging whoever had abused you. So I wrote a curt letter to my grandmother, demanding an apology, or I would cut off all contact with her. I felt uneasy afterwards, but the book said to expect that.

The only acknowledgement I had was via my sister, who told me my grandmother said she'd received a letter from me full of lies. So I stopped visiting her and, as I am the eldest, most of my family followed my example. My grandmother was in an old-people's home and I knew full well how keenly she would have

31

felt this. As well as cutting off contact with my grandmother, I also rejected other family members who didn't believe me.

Yet, because I was also practising meditation and cultivating spiritual friendships, it gradually became clear to me that cutting off from people did not work; it made me feel worse. At the time I had told myself that my actions empowered me. I'd convinced myself of this, so in a way they did. But in other ways I was deluding myself. First, if I'd thought deeply about it, I would have known the letter to my grandmother would never get a response. It was such an irrevocable deed. All I'd achieved was a release of my own feelings at her expense. Secondly, I was, in effect, punishing members of my family for not giving me their support, belief, and apologies. But these things cannot be demanded. When you aren't psychologically integrated you only feel your own suffering. You cannot consider the other person or even your own long-term needs. I saw that I had to allow people to make up their own minds and that I couldn't usefully issue them with the ultimatum, 'If you're not for me, you're against me.'

Following this realization, I decided to engage in the process of forgiveness. Here I had another insight. I had used to think that forgiveness was a once-and-for-all action. Now I saw it was a process, and that the most important thing was my intention. My intention now was to get back into relationship with all those from whom I had cut off. With an attitude of forgiveness, genuine communication becomes possible. It's not that I felt sexually healed and whole again and so could forget about anger and blame. In a way it was the opposite. I saw that the only possibility of healing was through forgiveness.

Even now, I still feel pain and I am still affected sexually, but that no longer gets thrown at someone else. I don't want to blame anyone. I see now that some of what I was doing was trying to take revenge. I called it healing, but the deepest healing can never come by that means. It may be important to fully experience difficult feelings around sexual abuse, but it is equally important not to see those feelings as the final stage of the process. When the Buddha declared that we need not feel angry even if we are being hacked limb from limb, he's not demanding the impossible. He's trying to tell us, 'If you think you have an excuse to hate, you have not understood my teaching.'

I began to think about my grandmother's own life. She had been born illegitimately, and at the age of two she was abandoned by her mother who sailed away to a new life in Africa. She was passed on to a foster mother whom she grew to love, only to be snatched away by her maternal aunt who discovered the foster mother drinking in a public house, which she thought immoral. Then, to her delight, her real mother called her to Africa. She set out full of hope, but she later said that she must have been a disappointment as she was sent away after only two weeks.

I also thought about what I'd gained from her. She made everything around her beautiful, and was an exquisite needlewoman and cake-decorator. She also played the violin. I'm sure she passed on some of these aesthetic sensibilities to me. Reflecting like this, I felt much more sympathy for her. It must have been terrible to have been treated like that and to have no family. In the end I concluded that she'd had a worse deal than me.

We normally only care about things that affect us. But as I tried to understand the conditions that made up my grandmother's life, I began to forgive. I had heard the aphorism, 'to understand all is to forgive all' many times, but now I started to understand it. Happy people do not act with cruelty. If someone has done something cruel, they were not happy. Although it may go against all our instincts, there is no sense in adding more hatred to that equation.

I also reflected on the Buddha's teaching that none of us escapes suffering. If we've been treated badly, we can often feel that someone must be to blame. Defining myself as a victim gave me a sense of identity that had previously been absent, and that made me feel stronger. Some of the therapeutic material certainly encouraged this line of thought, but it was not so clear or passionate about what might lie beyond it. The danger of this approach is that it can lead to a vicious circle in which, to maintain that sense of identity, the anger and hatred must be kept alive.

In contrast, the Dharma tells us that life is like this, and the most important thing is to realize that we are not alone. There is so much grief and suffering felt by all of us and caused by all of us. We can tend to stereotype people who sexually abuse children as evil monsters, and certainly not imagine that they might be women, who are meant to be caring and nurturing. But now I can see that they are ordinary human beings.

So although my grandmother caused me so much pain, when she lay dying it was me who asked her for forgiveness. If anyone had suggested when I'd just had the memories, or in the several years following, that this was the way to healing, I'd have thought it outrageous and probably got angry. It took patience and consistent practice to reach that point. Forgiveness is a process that cannot be forced.

A key meditation practice for me is the *mettā bhāvanā* (development of loving-kindness). It has been crucial to me to cultivate compassion and forgiveness for myself. Another aspect of this meditation involves developing *mettā* for someone you don't like, or who has hurt you. Sometimes, especially early on, I could not include my grandmother in this aspect. But I kept doing the practice and it began to work in its own way.

I still struggle with forgiveness and with giving up grudges. But in my heart of hearts I know that holding on to resentment means holding on to my own pain.

going inside

Suvarnaprabha
(Suvanna Cullen)

There is a series of rituals you learn when you start going into prisons. Of course, they aren't meant to be rituals; they're for security, but they end up feeling like rituals, in the same way that some of us automatically bow when we enter a shrine room. You walk up to the door, push the button, turn your back to the door, the door buzzes, and you turn around, open the door, and go inside. Every time you go through a door, even on the inside, you do the same thing: push the button, turn to face the camera, open the door, go inside.

A few years ago, I spent four months co-teaching a creative writing class at a medium security prison. Once a week I drove my little Honda into the hot Central Valley (where pretty much all California's prisons are), my chest achy and nervous every time. Walking in the first day, I passed through a series of remote-controlled gates, each buzzing as we approached it, someone watching us on a screen somewhere, pressing a button to let us through to the next gate. Even as a visitor, you feel you have no control over what's going on. At almost the last gate, the Director of Arts in Corrections mentioned that he was required by law to tell me that the prison policy is not to negotiate with terrorists. 'We're supposed to tell people before they come in,' he says.

That confused me. On the one hand, it was sort of exciting to think that someone was legally required to warn me that if I were seized by the neck and dragged away, nothing was going to be done about it. And then came the thought, 'It's too late to

35

run now, with all those locked gates behind me.' I felt I was entering another world – of wall-mounted cameras, hostages, and violence; a place behind a wall of electric razor wire, with its own customs and language, looked on with fear and hatred by those outside, perhaps including me.

In the US, about two million people are incarcerated, and the unfortunate news is that the experience tends to make them more violent. The current Sheriff of San Francisco was a prisoner's rights attorney at our county jail in the 1970s, when it was described as a 'monster factory'. He resolved to try to change it into a place that prepares inmates to rejoin the community, helps victims to heal, and helps communities to play a role in rehabilitation. Such a system is referred to as a regime of restorative justice. This is one of the most progressive jails in the US.

For the last five years, thanks to the Prison Meditation Network, I have been going to the jail every week or two with a yoga teacher. We do some yoga in a circle of about fifteen muscle-bound, orange-clad guys, meditate, then have a discussion about meditation or whatever comes up. The class is voluntary, and participants come from one of two restorative programmes: one is for drug-related offences, and the other is for those in a violence-prevention programme in which men confront the causes of male-role violence and work to observe, understand, and change their behaviour. The programmes, especially the one for violent men, are meant to provide tools for understanding their conditioning, and enable them to work more effectively with their minds and their anger. About half these guys are in for things like violence against their wives or partners, or going against a restraining order.

My sister recently said to me, 'I can't really see what the appeal is. I would never go into a jail – it would scare me.' It was pretty scary for a while (but only when I thought about it, not when I was actually there). Part of the reason I started this was for a change from the mostly middle-class white people that show up at our Buddhist centre, even though we're in a non-white, non-middle-class neighbourhood. The most annoying thing about privileged people, at least Americans, is that we haven't the slightest idea that we are privileged; we just expect things to be easy and to be happy, while so much of the world grinds on, often smiling, in the face of real hardship. So I like to get out of that sometimes, get a different point of view, and meditate with people whose level of engagement with meditation seems more like a necessity than just a trendy way to unwind. Plus, in a way, one's life and one's body are themselves a cage. I occasionally feel that, as the title of Bo Lozoff's book says, we're all doing time.

People who want to change, no matter where they are, are interesting. In a sense, the degree to which they want to change is the degree to which they are interesting. People who realize they have made mistakes and are trying to learn are interesting. They may have done – probably did do – horrible things, but when they are with us they are mostly receptive, kind, and appreciative, and I love them. It's just that many of them are covered with tattoos and have unbelievably huge arms. And after a while I stopped noticing that.

I walk to the door of one of the dorms with the yoga teacher. The deputy yells out to the crowd of about fifty men, 'Yoga and meditation!' A few guys shuffle up to the front. Most are clustered together watching a movie on a set high on the wall. Two African-American guys lean against the wall, missing teeth. I ask if they're coming to yoga and meditation.

The big guy says, 'What, is that like acupuncture?'

'Huh, is it like what?'

'Acupuncture, is it like acupuncture?'

'No buddy, we ain't going to use needles on you.'

'I know, like you know when we're sitting around in a circle, all quiet, but without the needles.'

'Yeah,' I say, 'it's like that.'

The skinny one says he'll come. I doubt it.

We reach the classroom, sit in a circle, and check in. One guy says he has toothache. Now they're doing yoga and I decide to opt out and meditate for an hour. Will I do it or won't I? There aren't as many old-timers as usual....

When they're done, I look around and say, 'We're going to do an experiment today, and you don't have to do it if you don't want to. First we're going to do something like singing, then we'll do a meditation on kindness. This kind of singing or chanting comes from a particular tradition, but I want to point out that I'm not trying to force anything on anyone, or convert anyone. I know some of you are Christians, and if you like you can think of this mantra as a prayer to God. So we're going to chant this phrase *om mahnee padmay hung*. It is a symbol of compassion – a symbol of human development – that sees people as flowers blossoming. So here goes: *om-mahnee-padmay-hung, om-mahnee-padmay-hung, om-mahnee-padmay-hung....*'

The white guy to my right starts laughing in an odd stop-start kind of way. I cringe inside. What if he doesn't stop? What if no one will join in and I am a failure? Can't turn back now. Another guy joins the laughing guy, who now sounds slightly hysterical. I am not looking but something is definitely going on to my right. Seems very bad.

I continue *oṃ maṇi padme hūṃ*, the magic mantra, deep. God help me, as it were. Five minutes, that's all we'll do, and if it doesn't work, it doesn't work. It feels very Buddhist to me, too much for this secular place. The sound fills the cold hallways. What if the deputies protest? Many people here are Christians.

Waiting, chanting. After about three minutes, everything goes still. There is only the mantra, deep and clear. My own mental noise has stopped, the laughing guy has stopped, no keys jangling, no doors slamming. Everything has stopped but this group of people, this rippling, low-voiced beauty. Everything changed.

After five minutes I ring the bell and the chanting fades. We cultivate an attitude of kindness towards ourselves, then towards all beings, including our enemies. The nervousness creeps back in. Is the meditation too long? I am worried about introducing the cultivation of love, awareness of emotion, here, after they've known only the Zen-inspired approach of 'letting go of thoughts'. There was some shifting around during the meditation but, during the last stage, in which we focus on all beings, everyone settled down. When people seem restless in the meditation, I have learned to take it less seriously. I figure it's better just to carry on. I ring the bell three times … the reverberations last a long, long time.

Some people take to loving-kindness meditation like fish to water. I understand these people. They look beautiful after they meditate, like they just got back from a retreat. The skinny new guy's eyes, when they open, look like he is in love, sparkling. I wonder if that was like acupuncture. I am careful not to stare at him. The white guy next to me says, 'I'm sorry I was laughing, I didn't mean any disrespect. I'm sorry. I don't know what was going on, I couldn't stop, I didn't mean any disrespect. I couldn't stop.'

The guy on the other side of him says to him, 'I'm sorry I got mad.'

'That's OK, I didn't like it myself, I was trying to stop but I couldn't.'

I tell him he can be kind to himself about having had that experience. It's fine with all of us. 'Yeah, it's fine,' they all say. Everyone looks so kind.

The yoga teacher explains the physiological benefits of chanting, according to the Hatha yoga tradition. I'm glad she can do that. It sounds sensible.

Someone said he found the meditation very difficult, which I took to mean that he couldn't engage with it. He said that during the difficult person stage, so many people flooded into his mind that he would get really angry about it, then he would get angry that he was angry, and so on. In a later class he said that his interactions with people had changed after he'd done the practice only once. He had never actually seen people as people outside of what he wanted them to be, and that he had started doing that. The change seemed tremendously painful – suddenly to have that kind of awareness, to realize how it's been before, and to see how much painful work one has to do.

I remember when I started, against my will it seemed, to become acquainted with the violence of my own mind. I was on my first week-long retreat, and in one of the meditation sessions, my whole experience, my whole being and sense of myself, sort of filled up with awareness of hatred, and I saw with an indescribable immediacy what was underneath so much of my experience. I saw how at some level I hated myself and other people. Of course I also loved people, but I didn't love them how I love them now. That retreat was excruciating, as were many subsequent retreats. The path to happiness can sometimes be sad.

'I really want to change,' an African-American guy says, another one who looked blissed out after the meditation. 'Thank you for coming here, thank you,' he says. People are very beautiful; I have to stop myself from looking at them. Some people end up getting out of jail and losing it – stalking their ex-wives, taking drugs again, both. Some of the yoga and meditation teachers get upset when this happens. Yet, I figure, doing some productive time isn't going to be enough for some people, perhaps most people, to transform a lifetime of addiction and violence. But while we're in the class, there is something else going on, about peace and acceptance, something that seems to be rare – anywhere in this world.

The new guy is still sparkling. Is he in love with me? Well, the anxiety seems misplaced in the face of this beauty. The other guy I had problems with doesn't come any more. This guy is different. He is a flower.

Shin, the monk from the Pure Land tradition with the big Sanskrit *āḥ* tattooed on the back of his head – whose master told him he couldn't give Dhamma talks in jail – tells me I was chanting it too slowly. He says the resonance is right when there's no pause. He looks extremely happy.

The guy with toothache says his pain's gone. Another guy says his headache has gone. Another guy throws his crutches across the room, stands up and walks. Just kidding – about that last thing.

The laughing guy says, 'You know, when he got mad at me, I just thought, "This is how people are, he can get mad, it's OK". There but for the grace of God go I…. I've never thought anything like that before.' He looked happy, and also shocked.

Everyone looks so kind. There is love in the room. Transracial, transpenal, trans-sectarian love – the kind you can't actually define. Devi and I are leaving now, both very happy, walking to the door, towards the big outside. And I say, 'Well, that mantra was great, but I won't do it again, or I'll wait a year or so. There's something not right about it here.'

I press the button and a man in a booth looking at me on a screen presses a button. The door buzzes and we are outside again. When I get home I am so happy I can't sleep.

dead man waking

Frankie Parker
profiled by Anna Cox

One day in 1982, in the small Ozark Mountain community of Rogers, Arkansas, 28-year-old Frankie Parker murdered his mother-in-law and father-in-law, shot his sister-in-law, and kidnapped his ex-wife Pam Warren. Then, in a stand-off with the police, he wounded a police officer. He had eavesdropped on a telephone conversation and heard that Pam wanted to kill him. They had divorced six months previously and he was in a desperate rage over her loss. Bolstered by massive doses of cocaine and alcohol, he decided to buy a gun and pay a friend to kill him, reasoning she would be suspected of his murder and go to prison. When that plot failed, he took the gun to her parents 'to frighten them'. The next day, he found himself in a hospital bed, woozy from drugs. The television was on and he watched a report of the previous day's terrible events, of which he was the cause.

Probably few were surprised. Frankie Parker had married and fathered his first son at 16. During a stint in the army in Korea he ran a lucrative sideline selling illegal drugs and black-market goods. He married again, had a second son, and then another divorce. Then he married Pam. When she, too, divorced him he ran wild with threats. The whole town knew about Frankie's craziness, but was still appalled by the murders.

Frankie Parker was sentenced to execution by lethal injection and went to the place that would be his home for the next twelve years: Death Row at Arkansas's Maximum Security Unit in

Tucker Prison. Appeal after appeal was filed, and Frankie fired lawyer after lawyer. He became known as a very difficult prisoner. The first four years were an unending cycle of attacks on guards or fellow prisoners, followed by vicious retaliation which further fuelled his bitterness. By way of punishment, Frankie was frequently thrown into 'the hole' – a dark cell with no amenities. He experienced the greatest hell realms, but could hardly recognize that he lived in them, much less see an escape.

On one visit to the hole, Frankie demanded to be given a Bible – the only book allowed. The guard grabbed a nearby copy of the Buddhist text, the *Dhammapada*, threw it into the cell, slammed the door before it could be thrown back out and yelled, 'Here's your goddamn Bible.'

Frankie yelled himself into exhaustion and finally picked the book up. He began to read.

Our life is shaped by the mind, we become what we think. Suffering follows an evil thought as the wheels of a cart follow the oxen that draw it.

Our life is shaped by the mind, we become what we think. Joy follows a pure thought like a shadow that never leaves.

'He was angry with me, he attacked, he defeated me, he robbed me' – those who dwell on such thoughts will never surely be free from hatred.

'He was angry with me, he attacked, he defeated me, he robbed me' – those who do not dwell on such thoughts will surely be free from hatred.

For hatred can never put an end to hatred; love alone can. This is an unalterable law. People forget that their lives will end soon.'

Frankie recognized himself for the first time, and the words indicated there was a way out. Those months in the hole were spent consuming the Buddha's teachings as though they were speaking just to him, and when the guard opened the cell door the text was indelibly imprinted in his mind. Leaving the hole, he passed through a series of security doors but he later commented, 'I escaped from prison when I began to practise the Dharma.' A year later, amid tears of gratitude, Frankie told the guard who had thrown him the book, 'You gave me the greatest gift I ever received.'

With more determination than he'd ever had, Frankie started waking at 3am. Following the directions in Boz Lozoff's *We're All Doing Time*, he tried to meditate. At first he felt he was just self-consciously staring at the walls, but little by little he found a stillness. Incidents that might have provoked anger started appearing as opportunities to practise mindfulness. The changes were slow, and he wondered if he was making any progress. Renewed determination came when, after about a year, other inmates started to comment on how different he was.

Frankie began to practise the meditative arts of origami and calligraphy, and in the exercise yard he taught himself t'ai chi ch'uan. The recreation one evening was a martial arts movie and, after watching it, his friends on Death Row told him he was like the guy in the movie. They teased him by calling him by the hero's name, Si Fu (teacher), and it became his new name. He suspected he had read every book on Buddhism in the prison library. He spent the $15 a month from his mother on books not available at the prison rather than other necessities. Frankie diligently educated himself, as thoroughly as someone studying for a doctorate in philosophy and religion. More importantly, he put the teachings into practice and – mindful moment by mindful moment – his heart opened in compassion and his actions became deeds of kindness. 'What is the greatest act of kindness?' he would later ask. 'A smile. Greet everyone with a smile. Meet everything with a smile.'

Living as a Buddhist on Death Row was a challenge. Yet his role with his fellow inmates and with the guards changed from the angry antagonist to a man who befriended those in the same pain he had once known. He read to illiterate prisoners and protected some who were mentally retarded. He joked with the guards and, in return, they came to trust and appreciate him enough to share their own dilemmas. When situations erupted that might have turned violent, Frankie often stepped in as mediator. Most of all he became notorious for the jokes he played on his friends. Death Row, they said, was a riot when Frankie was around. The warden told him, 'I wish all the prisoners were Buddhist if they could be like you.' Frankie commented later that he felt intensely proud that he had represented the Buddhist tradition honourably.

Frankie became the most powerful personality on Death Row, but for seven years he felt very alone. He had few visitors and most were Christian preachers wanting to convert him. His family were limited by money and distance and rarely came to see him. As a practising Buddhist, he assumed he was the only such oddity in Arkansas.

Although he had barely glanced at a newspaper in years, he happened to scan the religions page in the *Arkansas Democrat/Gazette* one Saturday morning in January 1994, and he came across an advertisement for a retreat sponsored by the ecumenical Buddhist Society in Little Rock. Straight away he dashed off a letter asking for support and help in his Buddhist study. I happened to be the Society's President at the time and I replied. As soon as my letter arrived he wrote again with more questions. And so it went on – eager but apologetic letters full of requests but hoping that he wasn't being a nuisance. There was no other way, he explained, that he could fulfil his deep longing for texts, instructions, and, most importantly, a Śākyamuni Buddha for his simple shrine. He already had incense and candles that he had made, a picture of the Buddha, and beads of multi-coloured plastic that a friend had strung for him. But he wanted a Buddha figure and the warden would only let him have a plastic one. 'I can't imagine why I can't have a metal Buddha,' he wrote to me. 'I guess they think I would use it as a weapon. Can't you see it in the paper – "Death Row inmate kills guard with Buddha statue"!' He eventually got his brass Śākyamuni Buddha after it had travelled with me from Nepal where I bought it specially, and had then sat for four months in the prison mail-room awaiting approval. Eventually, though, he was able to install it on his shrine.

I visited Frankie that spring. He was clearly delighted to have someone with whom he could share his passion for the Buddhist path, and we spent the three-hour visit discussing the Dharma. We talked about pain and guilt and chanted the purifying Tibetan 100-syllable mantra of Vajrasattva. We spoke about practices and meditations that he could do to prepare for his death, the thought of which never left him on Death Row.

In February 1995, Lama Tharchin Rimpoche, a Tibetan Nyingma lama from Pema Osel Ling in California, gave a teaching at Little Rock and he came with me to visit Frankie. The connection was electric and Frankie was ecstatic. Later he described it as the most important moment of his life. 'It was like a visit from the Buddha himself.'

Another year and a half passed and Frankie's appeals had run out. The execution date was set for 29 May 1996. I suspected we had some intense weeks ahead and I wanted Frankie to have all the support he needed. Although other sangha members were aware of Frankie and appreciated his many gifts, there were some fears about getting too close to him. But I urged people to write and also to go and see him. Once the visits began, the sangha were amazed at the qualities they encountered and in many cases an immediate love sprang up. Before long so many people wanted to visit him that the visits had to be carefully scheduled. A visit to this remarkable 'teacher' was a rare and wonderful blessing.

Kobutsu, a Western Zen priest from New Jersey, had spoken to Frankie on the phone and volunteered to be his spiritual adviser. He had immediately felt a strong connection to this inspiring man. Kobutsu began a campaign on the Internet to fight the execution. On 22 May, one week before the scheduled execution, Lama Tharchin paid Frankie a second visit. He gave him a teaching, and the *phowa* practice, which is said to optimize the chance of attaining Enlightenment at the time of death.

Meanwhile, Arkansas's governor, Jim Tucker, was deeply involved in legal scandals of his own connected with the Whitewater affair, and he was waiting for a jury to return with his verdict. He alone had the power to decide whether Frankie's sentence should be carried out or commuted to life in prison without the possibility of parole. Perhaps feeling it would be unseemly to execute someone while a jury was still contemplating his own situation, Tucker decided to postpone the execution. A new date was set and reset a number of times and finally fixed for 17 September. Tucker was found guilty and resigned his governorship. On 15 July he was succeeded by the new governor, a fundamentalist Baptist preacher named Mike Huckabee. Huckabee's first official act was to reset Frankie's execution date for 8 August, shortening his life by a month and a half.

Letters of appeal, including one from the Dalai Lama, had been flooding the Governor's office. Frankie also received letters of support and promises of prayers. Sanghas all over the world held special meditation days. But, as 8 August approached, it became clear that Governor Huckabee was determined to see through the sentence in order 'to alleviate the pain and suffering that the family had suffered for fourteen years'.

When Frankie's parents and sister saw him for the last time, the scene was remarkable. He was the one giving encouragement, even giving a teaching. He said he was not leaving them, only leaving his body. Sangha members and family visited until the day before the execution. He said his goodbyes. He often said those goodbyes were the hardest thing about dying. Our last glimpse of Frankie was of him being escorted, arms and legs shackled, across the prison yard to his 'death cell'. He could turn to see us but he could not return our waves.

On Thursday 8 August – a day when the temperature rose to 95°F – he was placed in a small, stifling holding cell. He meditated. He made final phone calls to his friends and family. Lama Tharchin called him from Switzerland to say goodbye and to review the *phowa* practice. He made origami animals and flowers for the guards and told them jokes.

As 9 p.m. approached, guards in riot gear came for him. He began to chant the Refuges. On hearing this they stopped, confused, until the administrator told them to continue. A small shrine with his brass Buddha was set up in a cardboard box outside his cell and as he passed it, tied almost immovably in chains, Frankie made three bows. Then he walked to the execution chamber, bowed to Kobutsu who had spent the last day with him, they hugged, and he walked through the door. He had asked that the last thing he saw should be an image of the Buddha, and a picture of Śākyamuni was held up for him by the Director of the Department of Corrections.

He was asked for his last words. 'I take refuge in the Buddha. I take refuge in the Dharma. I take refuge in the Sangha.' Then he looked at the Buddha image. At 9.04 p.m. Frankie Parker was dead. Frankie's final statement read, 'For eight years I have worked on kindling a small light of compassion out of the deep pain I have caused. This little light is now extinguished… I pray that others who have committed heinous crimes may find this small light an inspiration and may spread the flame of compassion to illuminate the entire universe, so that all beings may realize the fundamental compassionate nature that resides within us all.'

_____wasting time on death row

Jarvis Jay Masters

Perhaps a week after I heard the news of Rimpoche's death, I was escorted to the visiting booth for prisoners on Death Row in San Quentin, California. I sat there, looking through the window and trying to guess who my visitor could be. Who was taking the time to go through all the complications this prison puts one through in order to visit me? My thoughts drifted among all the people I hadn't seen for a while. And my tears welled up as the image of Chagdud Rimpoche came over me. I wished it was him coming to visit me. Then I realized how his physical presence would never again turn that corner and walk up to the glass window, as he had done so many times.

I adore him as both my teacher and my father. I thought of all the obstacles he had overcome to get inside this place to visit me, the hours he had to divert from countless others, hours he could have spent with an auditorium full of people wishing to take refuge within his presence and teachings. In the midst of my sadness, I knew how blessed I was that he had walked inside San Quentin prison to sit in front of me, on the other side of this very glass window. In later years, through all his illnesses, Chagdud rolled his wheelchair into the visiting room. He gave me my whole spiritual path, and I can now reflect not only on his continued teachings but also on his care and compassion.

Looking through the glass visiting window, I waited for my visitor to come. Thirty minutes passed, and I began to wonder if they had cancelled, but I stayed on, hopeful. The other inmates' visitors were already there, and I could hear conversations taking place around me.

My friend Russell and I were the only two people from the Adjustment Center who had been escorted to the visiting room that day. Russell, too, is on Death Row, and I've known him for about ten years. He told me he was expecting his baby sister. He wanted me to meet her, but somehow she walked past me without my noticing, and now she and Russell were already in the booth next to me. I could hear Russell's heavy voice talking into the speaker in the wall. He was telling his sister not to bring their mother to see him. His sister must have hit a nerve, because his voice was loud and serious, almost angry. His outburst caught my attention.

One of my biggest regrets is that I never saw my mother during the first seven years I was here – while she was still alive. Plus, I had just been thinking of Rimpoche and wishing I could see him again. So I was really thrown for a loop by Russell's remarks to his sister.

Why would he, several years older than me – maybe in his upper forties – not want his mother to visit him? The more I heard him angrily telling his sister how under no conditions did he 'ever, ever want' his mother to visit, the more I felt the old longing to see my own mother's face.

Russell's voice grew louder and louder. 'Don't you ever bring Mama up here. If you do, we're finished! That's it! I'll never speak to you again! I'd rather be put to death than to let Mama see me like this.' I thought of loved ones who had passed away while I was here, without me seeing them, because either they or I had somehow believed there would be a right time – a different time – when we would be together without a glass window between us.

No visitor ever came for me that day, so my mind was completely drawn into the dialogue in the next booth. And the more insistent Russell became, the deeper I fell, tumbling down into my memories and regrets.

With all the tears I'd shed and the deep pain I'd felt because of the lost chance to look into the eyes of my mother, I knew I needed to speak to Russell whenever I could. Though we are living on different tiers, and we are on separate yards, I figured I could speak to him through the yard fence.

It was hard to wait for the opportunity to speak with Russell. It took almost a week before I saw him on the exercise yard adjacent to the yard I was on. It had rained all through the night before, and it was a perfect, clear winter morning. Both of us were hanging out near the fence. For hours I held back, trying to find the words to get around the fact that I had eavesdropped on his conversation with his sister. Finally, I just stopped trying to find an excuse for listening, and I called Russell over to the fence. I told him I had heard him telling his sister never to bring their mother to visit him.

The first thing Russell said was, 'Yeah, Jarvis, I know you wouldn't let your mother come up here either. Man, it will be a cold day in hell before I let my mother come to this fucked-up place and see me like this.'

'Man, Russell, my mother passed away!' I said.

'Is that right?' said Russell. A sad look crossed his face. 'I'm sorry to hear that, Jarvis.'

'Yeah, Russ,' I continued. 'She died years ago, about the same time we first met. And to this very day I regret it whenever I think of the times she could've visited me. Every time I glance over at her picture on the wall in my cell, I wish I had seen her face in the visiting room. You know?'

'Is that right, Jarvis?' said Russell. 'You would've really wanted your mother coming to this shit-hole? To see you on Death Row? Being stuck in the visiting lines, talked down to by those some-times shitty-ass guards, and to see you for an hour at best man? Nah, man, my mother means way too much for me to even think about her coming to this rotten, fucked-up place – a place I got my own self into? Nah, and for what?'

'What do you mean, for what?' I interrupted. 'For what? Because she wants to, Russell! Because she bore you – not the other way around. Listen, Russell. There is nothing about this place, about you being here, about the clothes you're forced to wear – not even the fact that your bad-ass is sitting on Death Row – that can ever remove the son she is holding in her heart. She, too, is facing a death sentence, every time she thinks of where you are. She is waiting, hoping, praying you aren't executed. Every day she lives with the fear of losing you.'

'Man, Jarvis, I hear what you're saying,' said Russell. 'That's real talk, and I'm feeling it all, too. But hey, I've already hurt my mother way too much just by being here. She's an old woman now, in her eighties. And it would break her heart to see me like this. Shit! It's even hard to write to her, you know? Plus, man, you know more than anyone all the things these prison folks put visitors through. It ain't worth it, Jarvis. It just ain't worth it.'

'Russell, man, listen to me. I know it's discouraging. But it's not about protecting your mother. You don't want her to see you in prison, on Death Row, but this is where she has seen you since you've been here, Russell. You can't shield her from this fact. She knows you're here, dressed in state clothes, Russell. But she also knows how important her time is to both of you, Russell.'

'What do you mean,' Russell asked, 'about her time? I always tell my sister to let my mother know all the good chances my attor-neys say I have to win my appeal and get out of this place.'

'Oh, is that right?' I said. 'Then what happens if your mother, not you, is the one to die next week? Or next month? What then? What about everything you have in your mind that you've dreamed of saying to her – where would that go then? You see, Russ, it's not about you – you getting out someday – waiting and waiting for that. It's all about not letting time go to waste today, regardless of where we both can imagine ourselves tomorrow. Because there are no promises. I know this now, but I didn't actually realize it, truly, until that day the prison chaplain came up to my cell and stared into my eyes and said, "I have some bad news – your mother died."'

I began crying in front of Russell. 'And guess what I ended up being asked to do? Guess what took the place of everything I had dreamed of saying to my mother?'

'What? I don't know,' Russell said.

'You guess, Russ,' I said. 'You try to guess.'

'Man, wow, Jarvis,' Russell said sadly. 'I don't know, man. I can't even imagine my mother dying, let alone all the rest of it.'

'Well, I was asked to write something to be read at her memorial,' I said. 'And I'll tell you something. In every word my heart gave, in every sentence, every period I dotted, there were a billion more things in my heart that I wished I could've expressed to my mother in that visiting room. And if I knew then what I know now, I wouldn't have cared if the only chance to be with my mother was sitting on a piece of ice floating on the Arctic Sea. Because there never is a good time. There is only the time we have now, to make good our intentions.'

Russell and I just stood there, leaning on the fence. For a moment neither of us said anything. We didn't have to. I understood that until this moment, Russell had never let himself think about the fact that he could lose his mother while he was in prison. On Death Row the closest fear is your own death. This can consume you so much that everyone else seems immortal. It seems as if everyone you love on the outside is guaranteed to outlive you. I can't count the times I imagined myself out of prison and sitting with Rimpoche during one of his retreats.

For a moment, Russell just stared at me as if he had gone some place only he could go.

Then he said, 'Jarvis, man, I don't know what the hell I was trippin' on. All these years when my mother's been begging to visit me I had the nerve to tell her no. Man, I love that woman!' Tears welled up in his eyes. 'And man, I've been a real fool, a total jackass, you know?'

'No, Russ,' I said. 'There are lots of people – and not all in prison – who go about their daily lives with their mothers living in the next town, or only a phone call away, and the thought of stopping by or calling to share time and company passes. So they carry on with their lives, and don't make the memories that would support them, long after their mothers are gone. But being in prison, even on Death Row, can never erase all that there is to say and be with – if only you let your mother come to visit you.'

'Yeah, you're right, Jarvis,' he said. 'As soon as I get back to my cell, I'm going to sit down and write Moms a long letter. And maybe, just maybe, by Christmas, she'll be able to come and see me.'

'Well,' I joked, 'you're way too ugly to be a gift to your Mama's eyes, Russ. But for sure, she will be the best Christmas gift you will have gotten in more than ten years, eh?'

We both laughed. Luckily for me, both Russell and I did get visits on Christmas Day. I even had the chance to see Russell's mother. I noticed her when all the visits had ended – a short, smiling lady, still blowing kisses to Russell on her way out of the visiting room. She blew so many that I got me one or two of them, too. But more than that, I felt her love for Russell. And in that instant I realized the love my teacher Chagdud Rimpoche had felt for me. I watched his loving presence pass through us all.

being here

Vidyamala

Thirty years ago, when I was 16, I lifted someone out of a swim-
ming pool in life-saving practice and seriously injured my spine.
The injury left me with constant pain that has gradually wors-
ened over the years. This injury, and an additional spinal injury
in a car accident five years later, have changed me into a more
thoughtful person. I went from being an active, athletic young
woman who had not had to think deeply about life, into a
woman facing intractable questions about the nature of humanity, sickness, ageing, and the inevitability of human suffering.

My main area of inquiry has been exploring the distinction
between the unavoidable suffering that is a natural consequence
of having a body that will get ill and age, and the sharper suffering of reacting to this fact. Is this secondary level of suffering –
either pushing away unpleasant experience or blindly grasping
after pleasant ones – at the root of the restless unhappiness and
discontent we so often feel? How do we transform this knee-jerk
reactive momentum and create instead a sense of space and the
possibility of choice in each moment, no matter what our circumstances? Is this what the spiritual life is essentially about? Is
this the key to freedom?

In my case, the options are stark and immediate: do I have physical pain and mental misery, which is truly horrible, or do I have
physical pain and a sense of space and choice in my mental and
emotional responses? I cannot make the pain go away, but I can
change how I respond to it. The motivation for finding a

creative, positive response is extremely high. This need for creativity in our responses applies to all of us. It is just particularly obvious to me in my circumstances.

These are big questions, but ones I feel fortunate to have had to face, despite the inner struggles they provoked. I would never have had the strength to choose such intensity if there had been an alternative. Yet, in a strange way, the pain that is so hard to live with is the very thing that drives me closer to the truth of the human condition. That is what keeps those searching questions constantly alive. Sometimes I feel impaled on these questions about the nature of life and human suffering, but the more I grapple with them – probing them, taking them deeper – the closer I am to coming to terms with life, just as it is, and to finding peace and understanding.

Although I had experienced physical pain since my first injury, these deeper reflections on responses to pain didn't emerge in any conscious or urgent sense for ten years, when I became very ill. Prior to this I had never dealt with my condition nor faced it in a mature way. I lived in an invented reality much of the time that pretended the pain wasn't real and simply blocked it out with medication and unawareness. I was able to keep this up for a decade, but then, inevitably, came a time of reckoning.

I was 25 years old and in an intensive care ward with neurological complications and acute pain. I was plunged into a strange and frightening world. Perhaps the shock of what was happening shattered my defences for a time – I am not sure – but I had intense and vivid experiences that changed the course of my life. The way I perceived myself and the world suddenly altered, and I see my spiritual life, in any conscious sense, as having started at that time.

The experiences were so intense and vivid that I could not but be changed by them – and they have informed much of my questioning ever since. Of course, I did not sustain the acuteness of perception that arose in that life-and-death time, but the memory of those perceptions has driven much of my subsequent practice. Since then, I have been on a quest for truth, wishing to live more and more in harmony with the human condition in all its complexity.

I had four experiences in hospital. The first was when I understood for the first time the necessity of taking responsibility for myself. I was confronted with the medical reality that there was no wholly successful treatment for my condition and that at best I should think about coming to terms with it – 'management' rather than cure. It was the first time in my life that the concept of taking full and complete responsibility for myself held any weight. Until then, I had indulged the fantasy that my difficulties would just go away, or I bargained, or I lived in plain, deluded denial of what I was experiencing.

It was shocking and difficult to realize 'this is it' – that my life did indeed contain physical pain and limitation when I was only 25 years old. It was extremely hard to let this fact in, but even then I knew there was something liberating in beginning to acknowledge this; and I felt galvanized to make the best of my life. Looking back I could see that in avoiding responsibility for myself I had precluded the possibility of improving my circumstances because I had essentially been passive. It was vital to realize this.

The result of the second experience was that I made an active decision to move towards life. I woke up one morning and felt sort of distant and thin. I felt I could easily let go of my life if I so chose. I looked out of the window at the city of Auckland and it seemed far away and unreal. I felt gripped by a huge, existential choice. Did I want to live, and take responsibility for my life, or did I want to give up and die? I felt that if I had chosen death I really could have died. I don't know if this is actually true, but it was certainly metaphorically true. It is quite possible to be spiritually dead while physically still alive.

At this crucially important axis I made a decision to live, and my life has felt qualitatively different ever since. It is as if prior to that point I was alive because I hadn't got around to dying, but since then I have been alive because I have actively and consciously chosen to be. Some weeks later I remember driving along Ponsonby Road, a main thoroughfare in Auckland, and looking at my hands, alive and vital on the steering wheel. I became acutely aware that the next time I confronted death I might have no choice about the outcome, and I realized I'd better make the most of my life now that I had chosen to live it.

The third major experience occurred during one long, long night. This was when I glimpsed for the first time, with a shattering impact, the meaning of living in the present. I had had a medical test during the day that meant I had to sit upright in my bed overnight. At this stage I hadn't sat up for months because of the severity of my back pain. It seemed literally impossible and yet … I had no choice. I was between a rock and hard place.

I was in an intensive care ward, surrounded by critically ill people who were moaning and fighting death. It was like a hell realm. I had never been in this sort of situation before, so there was also the shock and bewilderment of unfamiliarity. In the midst of all this suffering, there I was, sitting up in bed, wide awake, wondering how I could possibly survive the next few hours, and willing myself just to cope.

I spent some hours on what felt like the edge of madness, debating with myself whether I could get through the night – one voice saying, 'I can't do this. It is impossible. I can't last until morning. I'll go mad.'

Another voice was saying, 'you have to' over and over again, for what felt an age. It was one of the most intense and demanding experiences of my life.

Then, suddenly, out of that chaos and tightness there irrupted a sense of lucidity that contained the message, again as a voice, 'You don't have to get through till morning, you only have to get through the present moment.' Simultaneously my experience completely changed. It was like a house of cards collapsing, and all that was left was space. Suddenly the moment had changed from an agonized, desperate, contracted state to one that was soft, full, relaxed, and rich – despite the physical pain.

In that second I knew I had experienced something real, reliable, and trustworthy. I also intuited that I would spend the rest of my life making sense of it. It contained such questions as, 'What is time? What is space? What is the past? What is the future?' But these questions came later as I considered the experience more conceptually. In the experience itself there was just a knowledge that much of my pain and distress were caused by my reactions and fears, along with a knowledge that I could be utterly free of these things. I also saw for the first time that 'the present moment is always bearable', and this continues to sustain me all these years later.

The fourth experience occurred some days later, and was the first time I clearly understood that it is possible to be mentally creative and work consciously with the mind in order to transform one's experience and perception – even in the grip of physical pain. It occurred when the hospital chaplain, an elderly Anglican, came to my bedside to offer help and guidance. I was not a believer in any sense of the word, nonetheless he gave me a tremendous gift. He took my hand and led me through a guided meditation in which I experienced peace and joy, even while in a lot of pain.

My curiosity was aroused by this initial experience of meditation, and after going home from hospital I had a very good social worker who helped me further that interest. With meditation I sensed I had been handed a key that could help me make sense of what I was dealing with. I spent a year or so lying for hours a day on my bed at home exploring my mind and its reactions and responses, while gradually physically rehabilitating myself. I attended the Auckland Buddhist Centre a couple of years later, and at last found a context in which to make sense of what I had uncovered. This process of exploration still continues some thirteen years later with the help and guidance of the philosophy and methodology taught by the Buddha.

As the years go by I'm clearer about what essentially I am working on with the 'physical pain practice'. It boils down to aversion and reactivity. I experience something I dislike in the form of physical pain, so I react with aversion – sometimes grossly, sometimes more subtly. It is as simple and destructive as that, and my moment-by-moment practice consists of trying to retrain this negative attitude and instil a more positive response.

This is what we are all up against in life. I happen to have back pain that makes what I am up against very obvious, but we all have aspects of our lives that we find unpleasant – from the sharp pain and bitter loss of the death of a loved one to the milder frustrations of being stuck in a traffic jam on a winter's day in a car without a heater. And we all have the basic tendency to push away what we dislike and thereby to increase the experience of tightness and restriction – pulling tighter the densely woven layers of unhappiness.

I was very fortunate to glimpse a more creative perspective in hospital all those years ago. My daily task ever since has been to transform my moment-by-moment reactions so that I can gradually cultivate a positive mental state even when my body is causing me trouble. We all have situations every day in which we can't make pain disappear, and we will have them as long as we live in this unstable world. But in this very instability we can always find freedom in our responses. We can change our experience of pain – be it mental, physical, or emotional – from a 'thing' we recoil from, into a dynamic and fluid experience of the rising and falling moments of sensations within a broad and gentle awareness.

Change comes slowly, imperceptibly, like building a mountain out of grains of sand. It is not easy. Sometimes I am shocked at how insistent and seemingly intractable the knee-jerk reactions are, how loud the voice in the middle of the night that says, 'I don't want this.' But one thing that gives me heart is the confidence and strength that arises when I am able to meet what is happening with honesty – even if it is difficult – neither cutting off from the experience nor indulging it, just letting it be there as a momentary experience that has space around it and choice within it.

It is said that when Atīśa, a great Indian Buddhist teacher, went to Tibet to teach the Dharma he took his tea boy along with him because he found him so irritating and difficult to get along with. Atīśa was concerned that he might not have enough irritants in Tibet and he wanted to maintain an edge in his practice. He wanted to see when he reacted and to release the energy tied up in those reactions. I am heartened by his story; it shows me how working with pain keeps me honest because the taste of aversion is never far away, so the opportunity to transform it is always nearby as well.

Looked at positively, I see my practice as learning to rest in the present moment and finding peace there. If I think of my experience of pain in the context of the past and the future, it is overwhelming and depressing. My present experience gets lost in fears for the future and sorrows about the past, and the quality is one of tightness and restriction. However, if I remember that the experience of pain only exists in this moment, then it has quite a different quality. The present moment is vast and multidimensional when one starts to experience it fully.

Say I am sitting with a friend in the sun. Yes, there is physical discomfort, but there is also the pleasure of being with a friend, the sensation of the sun, an awareness of the environment, feelings of love. It is interesting to see this. I think we often become miserable because we have an unwillingness to engage wholeheartedly with life as it is happening now and experience its freedom and abundance no matter what our immediate circumstances. The possibility of there being a spacious, beautiful quality to life is present in all circumstances for anybody. I am sure of this.

Another way of 'using' personal suffering positively is to see it as a moment of empathy with others who are suffering. For me, this is the most tender and fascinating aspect of living with pain, and it goes to the heart of our shared humanity. When I have been able to stay with my own suffering in the moment with a light and kindly touch, I have felt that I sink through the particulars of my own condition into an empathy with that which is universal. I feel in touch with all beings who suffer and I care deeply about them. We no longer feel so separate.

In the depth of that experience lies knowledge of what it means to be human. This is an intensely beautiful experience and an antidote to pride and thinking that somehow I should be the exception to human suffering. Instead of asking 'Why me?' I ask 'Why would it not be me?' My suffering is stripped of personal drama and becomes instead a straightforward expression of being human and alive in this world.

I have noticed over the years that it is common for people to feel they have failed when they experience suffering, resistance, or unhappiness. I find this interesting. I have certainly felt this myself, and it seems to have a particular effect on people who, like me, are following a spiritual path. Although it is often this very 'problem' of suffering that prompted us to follow a spiritual path in the first place, we seem to think we should have reached the goal before we have walked the path. We all too easily make the mistake of wanting and expecting our spiritual practice simply to erase life's difficulties. We can start to regard our spiritual practice as an 'insurance policy', a hedge against suffering. But this attitude will, in all likelihood, reinforce our delusion and even alienate us from our shared humanity.

If, however, we can learn to meet whatever we encounter with courage, dignity, and honesty, then our practice can become a real, gritty training that can help us engage with all aspects of the human condition, from the tragic to the beautiful, with an open heart. I find encouragement in the words of Ch'an master Yumen: 'Don't say, when some day the King of Hell, Yama, pins you down, that nobody warned you. Whether you are an innocent beginner or a seasoned adept, you must show some spirit! A little bit of reality is better than a lot of illusion, otherwise you'll just go on deceiving yourselves.'

engagement with fate

Nissoka

My childhood is full of memories of my grandfather. He was an upright man who loved nature. He bought me my first pair of walking boots and we would go walking in silence for miles across Dartmoor's barren expanse. In this silence I would think deeply about the world, exploring my young, uncharted heart. What better gift could a boy have? And I loved my grandfather for it.

Then, when I was about 14, everything changed. He became fidgety and irritable. His bright intellect faded. The family thought he had not adjusted to retirement and sent him for counselling. But things grew worse. It became embarrassing to take him anywhere because of his involuntary movements and irrational emotional responses. He became abusive and even started beating my grandmother. We were afraid. Why was he like this? We wanted to find a cure.

Finally, he was moved to a mental institution, and we visited him every weekend. His agitated body and gnarled face contorted as we tried to speak to him. He moved violently and lashed out. His mind was agitated too; he seemed possessed by something, as though he were a lost kite blowing in the wind, and we chased the loose string that was his soul. At this point my grandmother died, emotionally exhausted, from a heart attack that came as she sat in her armchair. She was 60 years old.

Then a letter arrived from a distant cousin in America. A relative had been diagnosed with Huntington's disease. We should check it out on our side of the family. We looked in the medical dictionary and needed no further evidence – this was what my grandfather had. Huntington's is a degenerative, terminal illness. Symptoms start gradually and lead to death within ten to twenty years. The early signs are depression, moodiness, and unreasonable outbursts of anger. There are also jerky movements and clumsiness, so it can resemble Parkinson's disease. When the illness takes hold more seriously, the jerky movements become like a wild dance. Walking is impaired and falls are common. Eventually there is loss of continence and bodily control to the point of being wheelchair-bound and then bed-bound. Speech becomes slurred and swallowing is difficult. Along with this come confusion, forgetfulness, and possibly violent behaviour.

My family's response to the news was mixed. Now we knew what had taken my granddad and that he wasn't responsible for his condition. The atmosphere of blame gave way to understanding and forgiveness. But Huntington's disease is hereditary. The genes are passed down at a rate of 50/50 through both men and women, so we knew that exactly half our family would end up like granddad.

It's hard to express the family feeling at this point. It is one thing watching someone you love deteriorate; it's another to know that next it will be half your family. As we reflected on our uncertain futures, the weight of the outcome was amplified by visiting my granddad, especially when he was moved to a home for people with Huntington's. He was the oldest there. There were many people in their thirties and forties, twitching, moaning, rocking backwards and forwards uncontrollably. Some were in bed, skinny and close to death. I often cried after visits.

It is possible to have a predictive test to see if you carry the gene. Most of my mum's generation had this within a year. My mum, her sister Jackie, and her brother Richard all have the gene. Her sister June did not inherit it. This meant that my two sisters and I were at risk. They were clear, and I have it. My daughter Harriet, now eight, is at risk and will be tested when she's over 18. My cousins were also tested; some don't have the gene, others are waiting to be tested. There are about fifteen different gene patterns: mine means there is a 32 percent chance I will have the disease by age 35; this increases to 70 percent by age 40 and 100 percent by 48. While waiting for the results of my test, my mind swung between fear, hope, and denial. I saw the illness like a demon: it was dark and creeping, yet it carried a surgical instrument so sharp it could slice with precision those it chose to attack.

On the day of the result I woke up remarkably calm. When the doctor said, 'Your test has come through positive, you have the gene,' I felt galvanized. I thought, 'Now is the time to practise the Dharma.' I saw granddad one week before he died. I sat alone with him. His eyes could open and respond to me. I sent him love from deep within, I held his hand and told him that I wouldn't see him again. I said how much I appreciated his being in my life, and introducing me to Dartmoor and a love of nature. I held a picture of the moors covered in snow in front of his eyes and read some poetry.

As I left the hospital I felt in harmony with the way things are. I had just done the most natural thing, watching someone enter the river of passing away that millions of young people have witnessed in their elders. I felt confident and alive. At other times I've felt impotent in the face of this overwhelming force that is ripping 'my world' apart.

When I see people in the street with developed symptoms of Huntington's or Parkinson's disease I feel overwhelmed and sometimes I go and cry alone, in the back of my van or in a toilet. Sometimes this sadness is linked with a concern that the symptoms are coming on. Queuing for a sandwich, I knocked over a tray; everyone looked at me and some muttered about my clumsiness. I ended up crying in the fire-exit stairwell. I'm getting better at not letting these fears get out of hand, but it is difficult.

Last July I was feeling powerless and despondent after a specialist said he'd detected possible symptoms. I went to a field and considered taking my life. I wanted to drift into a world without the fear of Huntington's. I sat for a while thinking about my friends. Finally it started to rain, on me and my empty beer can, until I was soaking wet. I confessed to Vajrasattva, the purifying Buddha, all my limitations and unskilfulness; most importantly I confessed my self-pity. I begged him not to let me take my life because of this ugly emotion of the powerless. Any action driven by self-pity leads down a dark path, and I don't want to be compelled into darkness. I walked to the car and drove home.

It has been seven years since we received the letter from America. My uncle Richard has had symptoms most of that time. My aunt looks after him and it is not an easy job. My aunt Jackie had the illness for a while and died last year, my uncle George cared for her. My mum is also in decline and my father looks after her. Recently he disappeared for a few days, and we were worried. It is so hard for him to watch the woman he loved dissolve away, and to try to find a more unconditional love.

Since the demon crept into our home I have tried to be a refuge for my family, even though it has been difficult for me as well. I try to be receptive and kind, approachable yet not frivolous around the subject, and to create harmony. Different people open up under different conditions. My father and I sometimes garden together or go for a walk; my sister Jo and I sometimes go to the pub – she can talk more openly when we are away from Mum. I'm surprised how often people don't talk to each other about things that really matter. We also go on holiday together, just to have fun, and we're getting to know each other better. Our future lives will depend on one another; we need to feel confident that we'll be around when someone has fallen on the floor or their backside needs wiping. We may need to serve each other physically for many years, and make important decisions for each other when we can no longer make judgements for ourselves.

Having Huntington's has led me to search my heart for a deeper response than the suffering the illness brings. I've had to learn that it's not personal: it's not just 'my' family being taken away, or just 'me' in pain. There's an ocean of suffering and what I experience is just a part of it. Talk to anyone and you quickly find the suffering in their lives – physical, mental, existential – even if they appear well. I now empathize with people much more. Having felt the pain of the world myself, I want to be an ointment for others' pain.

When Huntington's first took hold of my family, I was overwhelmed by a sense of loss, as if my future hopes and ambitions had been taken away. I had imagined myself getting older, having a long and healthy life. Now I was forced into a kind of midlife crisis at 25: 'If I only have ten good years to live, what do I want to do with my life?'

These reflections led me to stop working and spend time alone writing about my life, writing characters in a novel. I also wanted to spend more time in India. Each year I go to Bodh Gaya, where the Buddha gained Enlightenment. I love engaging in a season of practice, and helping other pilgrims to find meaning in their journey to the bodhi tree by running classes. I also want to spend more time with my family.

Great pressure pushes us to be our most creative. So I am trying to focus not on how I will die, but how I will live. Everyone has to face my questions at some point. Having Huntington's is like being bitten by a poisonous snake with which I am in a mythic battle. But everyone is struck by a snake. There is something universal about coming to terms with one's own mortality. If I lose sight of it, I am not truly alive.

I have had fears about my future. 'Who will I be when the symptoms start?' But I am confident that by working selflessly for others, deepening my connections with Buddhist teachers, and clarifying and concentrating my mind through reflection and writing, I will be prepared – however the illness grips me. Another concern has been, 'What if I am violent? Will the positive effects of my previous practice be destroyed?' It helped to talk with my teacher Sangharakshita about this. He reminded me that such actions, if they happen, will be non-volitional bodily responses to my dissolving brain, just as the blinking of my eye is non-volitional. Therefore it won't have karmic consequences.

Last year my family attended a conference of 400 people whose families have Huntington's. On Saturday night there was a disco. Young couples with uncertain futures danced together, and people with mild symptoms, unsure of their footing, were helped by loved ones. Others' symptoms were more pronounced, their wild arms flailing violently. A friend of the family whose wife had died two years ago danced with a care worker. My uncle stood alone for a while and then said goodnight; my aunt had died only six months previously. No one underestimates the size of the demon we all face, nor the courage needed to face it.

At the conference I gave a talk. I was nervous about talking in front of so many people, but the pain of saying nothing when I could help would have been greater. I said that the battle is in our hearts and that we can conquer the suffering the illness brings with love, generosity, courage, and an ever more imaginative response. Maybe one day there will be a cure, but for the time being there is nothing we can do about the illness itself. We have to surrender to it. But we can change our response. We don't have to experience fear, anger, frustration, and depression. These are not symptoms of Huntington's, but our responses to it. We can take the initiative: we can feel the pain the illness brings yet still respond with compassion. And knowing this brings happiness and freedom. I believe it was refreshing to hear a new voice in a world where people often look to science for a solution.

Sometimes I think of life as a piece of writing. If someone said, 'Say it in 5,000 words,' then we'd write a story. If they said, 'Say it in 500,' we'd write a paragraph. If they said we had only ten lines, we'd write a poem. We can say just as much, if not more, in a poem. I no longer feel I am owed long life or health. I realize life never belonged to me in the first place, and any day that comes is a gift; I have to make the most of it. Life is a poem and I want to make it a beautiful one.

pain and gain

Aryadaka

I was driving home one Sunday afternoon in January. The sky was filled with thousands of crows, all madly enjoying the windstorm that had swept into Seattle that morning. My wife Sandra was at the wheel as we rolled along the tarmac. 70 mile-an-hour gusts of wind were sweeping the crows, cawing in a wild abandon, above the trolley wires and the roadway leading to our home. I delighted in the crows' flight. There were no predictable patterns yet everything was in perfect harmony.

I was returning from hospital after receiving a liver transplant owing to end-stage liver disease caused by the hepatitis-C virus (HCV). The operation took place on 6 January and I had been released just ten days after the operation. I had most likely contracted HCV between 25 and 30 years ago – it is sometimes known as the sleeping dragon because it can take so long to progress to the point at which symptoms are recognizable. HCV is at least fifteen times more common than HIV and, as in the case of HIV, there is no definite cure. In a few years time the number of deaths in the United States from HCV will overtake those from AIDS.

A transplant is the last ditch effort to save a life. I had been on the waiting list for eight months and as time passed I knew I would not survive many more months without it. I had already been called to the hospital three times on false alarms. One of the calls, where I was to be a standby for the primary patient, had resulted in my being prepped and taken all the way to the door of the operating room where I was interviewed by the anaesthesiologist before being turned away and sent home exhausted by the nine-hour ordeal, both relieved and disappointed.

When, at about 10 p.m. on 5 January, I received a call telling me that I was once again to report to the hospital, I felt, 'This is it.' I lived close enough to the hospital to be able to walk there with my 17-year-old son, Sean. The night air was pleasant. Scattered clouds hung in the sky and a few stars shone to the east over the Cascades Mountains. We talked about impermanence and the uncertainty of life as we strolled the quiet streets leading down to Lake Washington Ship Canal and the Montlake Bridge. I had a strong urge to reassure him that things would work out for him one way or another even if I were to die.

We both knew there was a chance I would die during the operation, but the alternative was certain death. Dying from HCV is often so slow that one hardly notices the changes and symptoms until they become quite severe. One thing I was not aware of until afterwards was just how gloomy life had become at home for my family and how the situation was affecting my friends.

Sandra was already at the hospital. The entire process leading up to the operation went smoothly and I completely surrendered to my destiny. Time flowed seamlessly and easily, the health-care professionals were compassionate and efficient. Sandra and Sean walked with me as I was wheeled down to the pre-op room, where the anaesthesiologist hooked me up, with multiple entry points into veins and arteries. Sandra and Sean were turned back, and Sandra's face flushed with colour as she realized there was no going back. The last thing I remember was being handed a phone as I lay on the stretcher, and hearing her voice. I cannot remember much of what we said because the drugs had started flowing into my bloodstream. I did not come back to consciousness until nearly 24 hours later.

I dreamed I entered a dark cave where there was an obstruction that had to be removed. It was fatally dangerous: a hard, foul object whose removal would begin a process of healing, yet it had to be replaced with something healthy for the process to be completed. And when the obstruction was removed there was a crucial moment when the cavity was empty, which was a very dangerous time.

The first thing to come into my awareness as I began the long ascent back into full consciousness was a feeling of bliss. I could hear voices saying my name, 'Aryadaka', which seemed strange since none of the voices was familiar and none of the nurses or doctors knew my Buddhist name. It turned out that Sandra and a friend had been speaking about me as Aryadaka, causing the nurses to do a double take – did they have the right patient? Sandra reassured them and explained why I had two names, and they decided to use it. This had a profoundly reassuring and healing effect on me during the period of re-engagement. The experience was strong enough to make me consider changing my name legally.

I felt I was dwelling in a dreamlike reality, and I knew that something profound and dramatic had just occurred in my life to which I wanted to give my full attention. At about this time I had another dream-like vision. I was on the edge of the Sahara Desert just south of the Atlas Mountains. I was travelling across a very flat, open plain along a narrow track whose sides were strewn with wreckage and bomb craters. Though this debris was exposed to the elements, the dry desert air had preserved it for all to see for many centuries to come. As I approached a rocky ridge I looked back and saw just how exposed these craters and wreckage were; they represented all the unskilful actions in my present life, and I realized that I had nothing to hide (in fact, nowhere to hide). I saw up ahead a clean track and realized that, as I journeyed through life, by not hiding the wreckage of the past I could stop creating more wreckage in the future. The vision felt confessional and liberating.

My sight gradually began to return and I could perceive shadowy forms moving about the Intensive Care Unit. I was surprised how content I felt; I was experiencing a strong sensation of bliss which, under the circumstances, I could not have accounted for.

As my mind and sense-consciousness re-engaged with the world I began to distinguish the people who surrounded me: Sandra and Sean, and several nurses who were organizing the piles of tubing left over from the surgeon's work. It took them several hours to reduce this to just two strands. I had a trachea tube down my throat so I could not yet speak, but my desire to do so was almost overwhelming. I began writing in the air. What a relief when Sandra got a pad and pencil and I could scrawl words out even though I could not see. I indicated that I wanted the tube taken out. When it was withdrawn I felt a surge of energy which swept me into a state of rapture. I could not believe how good I felt having suddenly found a new life with this new organ in my body. I called it a happy liver!

One of the nurses asked me how I was doing and I said I felt blissful. I had to repeat it as she had never heard a post-op patient say this. The overwhelming urge to communicate stemmed from the sense of gratitude I felt towards the surgeons and the donor. I was also surfing on a wave of loving-kindness from friends all around the world. Now I wanted to return that loving-kindness and communicate my gratitude.

I felt I had entered a mystical realm where my mind had been kicked free of constraints; pain and time no longer existed; self-grasping was absent. Only once or twice before have I experienced such profound bliss as this return to life presented to me. I felt I had been embraced by a field of compassionate activity. No doubt a combination of the drugs and my renewed physical vigour had stimulated the experience. My mind felt lucid, with a depth in which I could recall my life at ever deeper and still deepening levels. Life was a flowing pattern of vibrations and consciousness, and I was aware of compassionate activity at a level I had never really been in contact with before.

Hallucinations, dreams, and waking consciousness blended into an experience contained within a field of compassion. For most of the following week I was immersed in various realms depicted in the Tibetan Wheel of Becoming. At times I experienced a heavenly realm made up of myriads of Buddhas and bodhisattvas. But this would suddenly flip and become a hell realm strewn with images of death, skulls and skeletons picked clean, corpses in various stages of decomposition, darkness, and fear.

I also entered realms of desire where images of sexual organs populated the landscape. Though at times I came close to feeling fear, I found that whatever insight I had developed through my years of Buddhist practice began to pay off. I could turn away from fear and delight in the mental display, taking neither the positive nor negative mental states as ultimately real.

Even before the operation, my Buddhist practice had become much more free and open than ever before. I find attempts at formal sitting meditation almost impossible since there is a background of pain, and I generally contact an underlying fatigue that puts me to sleep. Working directly with illness and the impermanence of this body is enough. I am more aware of things, though emotionally life is a roller-coaster ride. I really do not want to die. I thrive on direct sensory experience, and now I feel more connected, yet less attached, to the phenomena of the world and the senses.

Immediately after the operation I felt I was dwelling in a realm in which everything had its place and it all fitted together perfectly. I so much enjoyed other people and I felt a tremendous desire to see others happy. I was delighted to be alive. I knew in the back of my mind that this exalted state could not last, but the experience of coming back to life, along with the attendant feelings of bliss and rapture, lasted for six weeks. I needed very little sleep. I was as happy as I had ever been in my life.

An organ transplant means that a person has come very close to death. In fact transplants are given only to those who have no other recourse in the attempt to sustain life. Since the transplant, I have had some big shifts in my outlook. I know I must find a more meaningful way to live. I have been having serious complications for the past two months, which have naturally come as a disappointment. It is still unclear exactly what the problem is, but the new organ is not functioning quite right and I have had many tests as the physicians try to understand what is going on. It has never been clearer to me how tenuous life is – and how precious.

This new perspective on life compels me to reassess my priorities. I want to spend more time with my family. I want my work to be more meaningful. I have managed to get a part-time position with the State of Washington Department of Corrections as the Buddhist Chaplain, which is a historical first. I am looking forward to this work, having been in prison myself for 22 months in the mid 1970s, when I began to take meditation seriously. I just hope I can find the energy to do it. I have an overriding urge to give something back to the world, and at the same time to take better care of my own needs and the needs of my family.

Many people ask me what I think of the person whose organ now resides in my body. I have thought about this a lot and I have no conclusions. Certainly a donor and a donor's family are people who consider life as a gift and look at ways of alleviating suffering for others. Organ donation is a great gift of generosity in the face of great grief. The organ donors and families of donors are the true heroes in saving lives. I hope to write to the family one day when my situation stabilizes.

I realize my life will never be the same. My appearance is different. I have a two-foot long scar across my abdomen. I am growing more hair, and my face has become rounder from the steroids (a 'moon-face'). I was told several times that transplant is no cure, it is just changing one disease for another. I now find it difficult to do many of the things I used to identify with. Will I ever climb a mountain again, or spend a summer's afternoon in an alpine meadow? Will I be disappointed if I cannot do those things?

I have found myself greeting strangers more often, and talking especially to those who are unwell. I am making attempts to come out of my own suffering by showing concern towards others I meet at the hospital who are struggling with life. I am fascinated by the way people cope with extreme suffering and situations of long-term illness and pain. I find it inspiring when I meet someone who is really making the best of a pretty awful situation.

I recently observed a young African-American who was confined to a wheelchair; he had lost both legs up to his hips, yet he was spreading joy and happiness wherever he went in the hospital. He was an extremely attractive person with kind words for everyone he came into contact with. I want to follow his example.

I want to become a kinder person through this final period of my life. Right now life is tenuous, but there is still a chance that things will be sorted out before too long. I am told that on coming out of surgery I was in the top ten percent in my response; now, these last two months, I am in the bottom ten percent. I hope the complications are sorted out. I want to give back to the world some of what I have received.

sacred service

Vajrashraddha

I had worked at the funeral parlour for only a few weeks when I dressed little Emily. She was 81 years old and had no friends or family to go to the funeral – just a couple of staff from her care home could attend. She was 4' 10", and tiny, tiny, tiny. A sunken green belly, sunken eyes, sunken mouth, skinny discoloured arms, wafer-thin hands. I stroked them for a long while. The fact she was dead didn't stop me. It matters. She was cold because she had been kept that way to stop her from decaying more, but her hands were soft and the wrinkles had eased a bit. Her white plastic sheet was removed and I dressed her in a white satin gown. I liked the simplicity of this. It was odd to see a dead person in their 'finery' with ticking watch and hard leather shoes. Robin, my boss, said 'Bless her.'

I often wonder how I've come to work in the area of death and dying. Why is it so important to me to spend my time with people who are terminally ill or dead, and the people who care for them? To answer that I need to go back seven years to the person I was when I climbed down onto Kingcup, the boat on which my Dad had lived for many years. Dad didn't take great care of himself. He would leave piles of stuff on his bed and when it was time to sleep he would push it all to the end and climb under the blankets with the bundle on top, like a badger in a sett keeping warm. Now I was scared of what I might find, and worried about clearing up his things alone.

Earlier that day his friend John had phoned my mother from Spain to say he had found Dad in bed, dead ... of a pulmonary embolism. Strangely, the news came as no surprise to me, even though none of us were expecting his death. He hadn't been unwell. He was 67, the same age as his father when he died.

I also felt incredibly sad that I hadn't acted on the impulse I had felt – for a couple of weeks – to write Dad a poem expressing my love and gratitude. I'd never said it when he was alive and now I had missed the opportunity. I had put it off until tomorrow, and now there was no tomorrow. I learned the hard way.

Looking back, I think that with my father's death I started to open to the reality of death. I wonder if we have to 'experience' a death or witness someone dying we really start to feel the truth of impermanence. Then the knowledge that all things are impermanent may shake us to the core.

I was impressed and grateful to the man who arranged my father's funeral, and I decided I wanted to help others who were experiencing the loss of someone close to them. That, I realized, was my vocation – something I desperately wanted to do before I died. Shortly afterwards I began training to be a funeral director, and my wonderful boss let me gain experience in any area I wanted, whenever a suitable opportunity arose.

One part of my work was to arrange the funerals. The bereaved relatives I encountered were not only trying to cope with their shock and grief, they also had so much to organize. Some were in a daze. I helped to arrange a dignified and fitting ceremony to mark the end of a precious life, and enabled people in distress to gain some clarity in a time of great confusion.

When someone loses a loved one it can be agonizing, even overwhelming, and leave the bereaved feeling that life is not worth living. Sometimes they cannot see how to get through the day. This is a natural and honest response to having loved and lost.

Occasionally I hear people suggest, on learning that a friend has lost someone close, that this is an opportunity for spiritual insight to arise. Maybe so. But we cannot short-circuit grief. Only when we have felt the loneliness of a broken heart in the pit of our bellies can we fully understand it.

The aspect I found hardest was arranging funerals for people who had no one involved in the planning and no one to attend the funeral. I once carried a coffin containing the leathery skeleton of a man who'd been dead for eighteen months. It was pitiful to imagine a life so lonely that nobody had even noticed he wasn't around for a year and a half. How can we live in a society so fragmented that this can happen?

The other part of the funeral parlour work was caring for the deceased. A decomposing corpse is not a nice sight and can smell foul. I made a practice of remembering this was once a human being, which helped me to overcome any sense of revulsion. I felt a need to care for the dead tenderly and treat them with reverence and respect.

Death is a mystery – we cannot be sure what happens afterwards – but I don't believe it means total annihilation. In my experience, consciousness seems to linger for a while and it has always felt natural to me to talk with the deceased or stroke their hand. I know their body is a lifeless, breathless, rigid shell, and they cannot feel my touch, yet doing so somehow feels like an act of devotion. It has kept my emotions flowing and I have grown fond of many people I've cared for.

My main desire is to communicate with those who have been touched by death, whether confronted by their own death or that of someone close to them. It was this, together with my sadness at the thought of people dying alone, that led me to work as an auxiliary nurse at St Christopher's Hospice. My duties are quite practical: straightforward tasks like giving patients their food, talking with them and their families, making beds, cleaning dentures, emptying catheter bags, or pushing a patient in a wheelchair around the garden. But I find myself engaging in all this with a feeling of 'serving' people who are so in need of kindness.

My work team is an extraordinary group of 'guardian angels' and our task feels beautiful, meaningful, and true; about as true as it gets. I find it both sobering and uplifting. Taking care of someone close to death is a sacred act in which certain boundaries are dissolved and each of us is affected by the other. Communication is typically immediate, intimate, and honest. The people I meet are often full of fear and a tremendous sense of loss: loss of control, loss of identity, loss of certainty, loss of companionship, loss of lifestyle, and, most devastatingly, loss of life. Simply bearing witness to this can help to alleviate their fear.

I sit with someone and allow them to cry, without becoming embarrassed or trying to make everything all right. Paying someone full attention at this time seems to work magic, and a deep trust can quickly develop. Within minutes of meeting a new patient, I can feel as if they are a part of me, part of my life.

Situations change quickly and every hospice shift I work is different. I've learned not to assume I know what a person will be like when I enter their room. Patients' moods can swing rapidly, energy comes and goes, lucidity and vagueness regularly alternate. Patients are often too weak to say what they need or want, but if I listen with my whole being, even without words the person lying before me is able to express themselves. Silence, eye contact, or touch are often medicinal. A kiss, a wave, a smile, a tear, breathing together, holding hands.

This constantly changing situation is a challenge. It is humbling to attend to a patient with whom I've built a strong connection over a few days, only to be asked on another shift 'have we met before?' Then how rewarded I feel if a patient's face lights up when I walk into the room and they reach up to touch my face.

And how inadequate I can feel when I have no answers to the questions I'm asked.

The only other time I experienced this kind of communion with a stranger was when I came across an old man lying on the pavement in a pool of blood. He was conscious in an unconscious kind of way, and when I crouched beside him I realized his brains were spilled onto the pavement. I stayed with him, cradled him, and reassured him until the ambulance arrived. His name was Eddie. While I was with him there was no separation between him and me. I felt no sense of shock, just completely soft and accepting. At that moment I accepted that life means suffering and that we are all interconnected. Soon afterwards the shock hit me, and I was deeply disturbed by the event. Eddie still feels part of me.

Death can shake us to the core and wake us up. When someone has advance warning of death, they often reassess their lives and make big changes. I went into this work to care for others, rather than to gain insights into death, but the more I experience death, the less I dispute the law of impermanence, and the more I feel a deep, unsettling vibration within myself that feels like the truth. I accept that truth, I have faith in it – while simultaneously not wanting death to happen. On the whole I hope people don't die, unless it is a release from chronic sickness, or the frailty of old age. Yet I don't see anything wrong with death itself. It seems completely natural, the only inevitable aspect of life, part of the constant flux and flow. I regularly ponder this apparent contradiction and wonder if the reason I don't like it when someone dies is that it takes me a step closer to reality.

I'm not conscious of being afraid of my own death, but I do fear the prospect of a lot of pain. Sometimes people's bodies bring intense suffering. This raises the burning question, 'Why does it have to be like this?' Yet I am amazed and inspired by the dignity of so many patients, who are often incredibly brave, uncomplaining, and grateful.

Grace was younger than me. Her athletic body had not responded well to breast cancer treatment. Her family clubbed together to pay for her to come to Britain for further treatment and, leaving her husband and six children at home, she came to the UK alone. But when she arrived surgery was out of the question, and then the chemotherapy didn't work. By the time she reached St Christopher's she was terminally ill. She was too weak to travel back home, and her family were unable to visit. They never saw her again.

Grace touched every one of our hearts, not only because it was so tragic that this young woman would never kiss her little children goodnight again; but also because she shone with such radiance. She became weaker and weaker, and her pain grew more constant. She was in danger of dying from an unstoppable bleed, her right fungating breast rotting day by day. But her spirit was so alive, her face lit up and her eyes sparkled as I walked into the room. I would sit by her bed and we'd listen to the sound of Taizé, the Christian community, chanting on the tape-recorder. It was like the sound of angels filling the room. I'd stroke her bloated hot arm. During her last week she was unable to speak, yet her silence shone. One day I came to work and her bed was occupied by someone else.

I am drawn to this work because it is intrinsic to life. It is liberating to know I cannot control life – that life and death are my masters, rather than I theirs. That death is a mystery and beyond control intrigues me. I have felt more alive working in the funeral parlour and the hospice, because of the ongoing reminder that it could be me on the deathbed. I'm more in touch with a desire to live well and make the most of these too brief times.

When I visited India a few years ago, death was publicly on display. At Varanasi, six bare-foot children escorted us to the burning ghats, holding our hands like protectors. There at the river-bank we saw long rows of corpses lined up on stretchers, according to their sex and age, draped in coloured cloths and flowers. The bodies were ritually dipped in the filthy, infested water to purify their souls. Funeral pyres littered the area, fires blazing, flesh melting, bones turning to ashes; the eldest son of the family circumambulating the parents' blazing bodies, sprinkling holy water and chanting all the while. No women were present, they are banned from the area because in the past some wives would become hysterical and throw themselves on top of their husband's pyre.

Amid all this paraphernalia were men who make their living by diving into the water to sift for gold and silver that may have been thrown into the River Ganges with the ashes of the deceased. Seeing these fellows scavenging in the disgusting filthy water felt more grotesque than witnessing the bodies crackling in the dancing flames.

We watched in silence for a long time. Witnessing it all was deeply sobering; at the same time I experienced tremendous stillness and relief. Amid the noisy hubbub of the area, there was also a sense of tranquillity. The children who had brought us were as familiar with it as any child with their own back garden. To them, the sight of death is as natural as the air they breathe. That evening I sobbed in my meditation and experienced again a wave of relief.

In the West we are adept at ignoring or covering up the simple but profound truth of death. We tend to live so far removed from an acceptance of death in our culture. I am regularly asked if my work is depressing. And many people refer to death as though it is morbid or, worse, a subject to be avoided altogether.

Discovering this vocation has enriched my life immeasurably. It has changed me in numerous ways. I am so glad to have nurtured the seed that was sown when my father died. It is showing me I have a heart that cares, and helping me to find the courage to dance amid life and death.

facing death

Shubhavajri
interviewed by Nagabodhi

When I was first told I might have cancer, I was completely stunned. I remember the doctor asking if I had any questions. There was only one that came up – how long have I got? And I didn't even ask it. People kept asking how I felt, but I just didn't have anything to say. I felt quite blank. I was stunned – as if someone had hit me over the head with a hammer.

My greatest concern was, 'How am I going to tell my mother?'

I have always seen death as part of life. When I was a child I would stop playing and count to ten and think, 'I'm ten seconds older; ten seconds nearer to death.'

I was offered a choice of treatments. I could have opted for a harsher treatment, which might have a slightly better chance of success, but with awful side effects: nausea, ulcers, and so on. The deciding factor was my quality of life. I knew I could go out and fight it 100 per cent, but what would my life be like while I was doing that?

Death is an important part of my life. When I was 17 my great grandmother died, and I wasn't told. Then, when I was at college, both my grandparents died, and I was only told when I came home for Christmas. I remember basically being told, 'Keep away from death and funerals because they are such awful experiences.'

When I found out I had cancer, the two words that came up were 'real' and 'true'. That was how I wanted to be with other people and how I wanted others to be with themselves and with me. If by what I am doing or the way I am others can look at their own deaths, or how they relate to death, in a sense that makes it all worthwhile.

My dominant preoccupation is with death. My death is imminent, although I don't know when it might be. It might be a month, it might be a year, and I don't even feel ready to ask which. But now I see my life as being about preparing for death.

When I was 26, my boyfriend died in a motorcycle accident. I remember thinking, 'It's different for old people, but young people aren't supposed to die.' It was as if I was experiencing for the first time something that had been hidden from me, and that I shouldn't have been experiencing.

I see death as part of a natural process in life. In the West we hide away from it. We come up with phrases like 'she has gone to sleep' or 'she has passed on'. It is such a great shame; it is so unnatural and unhealthy.

I have been through dramatic changes in these two months. From the start I noted how much more I needed to live my life in the moment. I have tended to be a planner, and think about what I am going to do in the future. I have always missed being in the moment and never really understood what people meant when they spoke about that. I have found I am actually experiencing what is going on, having to take one day at a time, and not even worrying what will happen next year. Even if I plan something, anything could happen. So I can't control what happens in the future. All I can do is live here and now.

One friend told me, 'I wouldn't have wished this on you but, in a way, it is just what you needed.' I understood what she meant, and I agree with her completely. Within days of the news it became apparent to me that I was quite different. I started living my life wholeheartedly.

I am learning that I need to ask for what I need. I have always been very independent, so I find that difficult. But now I do need other people and I can't do this on my own.

I feel happier now than ever before. I can't get my head around that. It is because my life has been cut down to simplicity by necessity. This moment is all there is. That's all I need to concentrate on, and that gives me great happiness.

Most people have been 'real' with me. That is what I find most helpful because it means we can talk openly and be honest with each other.

I saw clearly that this was a chance for me to develop all the things that people had been saying for years I need to develop, but I'd resisted, or thought, 'all right, but maybe later on.' Here is an opportunity, and how foolish it would be for me not to use it to do what I need to in order to grow.

I see others' mortality more clearly, and I can get quite frustrated if people talk about trivia or things they are looking forward in two years' time. I think, 'You might not be here in two years. What about seizing this moment wholeheartedly?'

My life is still an unfolding mystery. But a few years ago it became obvious that death was a theme running through it. It's so interesting – as if for me death is the purpose of this life.

I passed through a stage of envying people who have several more summers. That was part of the process of accepting that my own death is imminent; those feelings may come back again.

When the cancer was diagnosed, I had a strong desire to surround myself with beauty. So I asked people to put lots of flowers in my room. The Buddha of Beauty, Ratnasambhava, became very present to me.

The focus of my meditation is different because it feels important to address the area of pain, working on the physical level of stress and tension in the body; and being kind to myself. One phrase I find helpful is 'surrounding my experience with kindness'.

Death is something we have to do alone. I can have all my friends around me, but at the moment of death I have to face it alone. I find that quite scary. Since the diagnosis, people have made sure I'm never alone. But I think it is important that I spend time on my own.

I do believe in rebirth. It seems to make sense. Seeing how in this life I set up conditions and the consequences follow; why should the process finish at death? But I don't find myself thinking about rebirth. Whatever happens at death will happen and I can't determine that. All I can do is come back to the present and set up the right conditions here and now.

In an ideal world I would like to think that everyone was living as if they knew they were dying. So what I would say to other people is, 'Always live your life as if you were going to die.' I remember hearing that idea when I first came across Buddhism and I took it on board, but then I lost it. I have certainly taken it to heart again.

_____*struggles with the dragon*

Robert Hirschfield

My father's body lay curled up like a ball of wax outside the bathroom. My mother was busy eating her Sabbath chicken in the kitchen.

'Have some chicken,' my mother said, dislocating a drumstick. She had forgotten whose body was lying on the floor on the other side of the wall. But that morning her memory had leaped across the chasm. A dead body must not be moved on the Sabbath! Dad would have to stay put until sundown.

A friend had just given me Joseph Goldstein's *The Experience of Insight*, the first book on Buddhism I'd ever read. That led me to read still more books on Buddhism, in which I learned that in olden days young monks were sent off to charnel grounds to contemplate corpses, so as to drive the teaching of impermanence deep into their bones.

Lowering myself into a cross-legged position, I sat staring at my father's cratered buttocks beneath his soiled whites. (A two-pack-a-day Pall Mall smoker, he had died of lung cancer during the early days of my mother's illness.) I felt desolate and heroic – surprised to find myself still breathing in this space where breathing had stopped. The mystery of a space turned into a corpse. The absence of a man who had never been present. A man of impenetrable silences, who would plunder the sports section of the newspaper to the exclusion of war, fraud, famine, the tears of the world.

As an untrained meditator, I wondered vaguely if this act somehow linked me to the monks of the charnel grounds. A single taste, and I was hungry for lineage.

En route to the bathroom, my mother stopped to shoot a quizzical look at the corpse. The face was familiar, but the context threw her. She, with her Alzheimer's, was having the same effect on me.

'Don't step on your father,' she said.

Seeing her in her big empty bedroom, searching for her husband, her stockings, brought to mind the famous words of Suzuki Roshi that were then new to me. 'To give your sheep or cow a large, spacious meadow is the way to control him.'

In space, she was always tripping over time, puréed with losses.

'Where is dad?'

'Dead.'

'Where is papa?'

'Dead.'

'And mama?'

'Dead.'

'Who is alive, then?'

I'd go down the survivors list.

Where am I? I'd ask myself. In hell. A tiny space in which all the grass has been burned away. Suzuki was trying to grow a new patch for me.

> The only effort that will help you is to count your breathing, or to concentrate on your inhaling and exhaling. We say concentrate, but to concentrate your mind on something is not the true purpose of Zen. The true purpose is to

see things as they are, to observe things as they are, and to let everything go as it goes.[*]

I'd look at that last line with a hard squint. When my mother was not hiding dollar bills inside her tissues, or imprisoning her dinner in the refrigerator, she was mistaking living relatives for dead ones, and night for day. I was there to extricate and disentomb, to illustrate and explain. It was like wrestling with wild air. But to let go? I was too busy waging jihad against hideous change to let go.

Suzuki's words did not let go of me. While pointing furiously to the sunlight on the sycamore tree as proof that it was day and not night, I'd think, there's got to be a better way. And one day, when she said, 'It's so dark out,' (it was a bright spring day) it occurred to me that maybe she sees the darkness outside as a reflection of, or as an extension of, the darkness inside.

I turned her away from the young leaves she was gazing at in terror. While reading *The Experience of Insight*, I drew my first ever conscious breaths. The event took place on my new, sky-blue *zafu* (meditation cushion). Such a simple thing, really noticing that I was breathing. Breathing in, breathing out. How flagrantly simple compared to my mother's terminal confusion, which extinguished the great light that once inhabited her eyes. After the dear, doomed trajectory of our story, simplicity. The discovery of a silent space where the weary dance could come to a full stop.

Not that it often did, of course. More often than not (far more often), the dance was the meditation, the meditation was the dance. How could it have been otherwise? The poisons of guilt, rage, regret sat there with me on the cushion – world-class hindrances that cut me no slack.

'Bobby, what are you doing down there?' she'd ask.

[*] Shunryu Suzuki, *Zen Mind, Beginners Mind*, Weatherhill 1999, p.33

'Plumbing,' I wanted to say. Trying to clear a path. From time to time, I would come upon shafts of silence, of clarity. Paths being cleared. Dharma gifts. They astonished me, even though I'd read about that in the books – I thought silence and clarity were things that happened to other people.

I recall her once asking me, while I was meditating, 'Aren't we going shopping?'

It might have been the seventh or the tenth time she had asked me that. I have chosen suitably cosmological numbers because the question, instead of meeting the usual daggered resistance, orbited in the allowing space that the silence had created. Inadvertent tormentor morphed into disassembling whisperer.

I took my mother to the little grocery owned by a squat, clean-shaven, Hasidic survivor of the concentration camps, and his squat, wigged wife. Years later, in John Bayley's Alzheimer's memoir, *Elegy for Iris*, I was struck by the words of an Alzheimer's spouse to the author: 'Like being chained to a corpse, isn't it?' I'd often felt that. But that day my mother was light on my arm. I'd have a long wait before she was that light again.

The grocers greeted her warily. (Gone was the exuberance of the old days – the casualty of chickens ordered and forgotten about.) Across the marble counter, the three of them used to return at will to the Jewish ghostlands of Eastern Europe. A few zany mouthfuls of Yiddish and muddy streets would stir once again in the borough of Queens.

These days the dialogue between them was stripped bare. A polite, 'So, you are out shopping with your son,' on their part. A simple request for a package of cheese on her part.

My confrontation, as a new Dharma student, with Alzheimer's, was a mismatch – rather like asking someone who's just learning how to swim to tackle the English Channel.

I came to think of Alzheimer's as the charnel ground of the mind. A fire that incinerates light. A fire that darkens what it has darkened. For seven years I sat beside that fire, my first teacher. It periodically burned awareness into me like a good teacher should.

How to describe it? The sadness, like mould, that would settle in the throat, in the defeated marrow of the bones. The sadness that was always there, a kind of implanted musical chord that was sometimes high, sometimes low, and sometimes silent, like the blood running through our veins is silent.

The sadness was especially strong when I was about to enter her house, or when I had just left. On the one side of her door, her absent presence; on the other, my pulverized love, my desire to be with her, to be gone from her. My desire for her never to go, my desire for her to be gone.

_raising the stakes

Andrew Black
profiled by Vishvapani

The World Series of Poker at Binion's Casino in Las Vegas is down to its last five players. After eleven days at the table, little sleep, and ferocious competition, they are the last survivors of the 5,000 people who each paid $10,000 to enter this no-limit hold'em tournament. The winner will walk away with $7.5 million. Behind designer shades and $21 million in chips sits Irishman Andy Black, nicknamed The Monk following his five years out of the game living a Buddhist life in the UK with the FWBO.

With a $1 million in chips already bet on this hand, Steve Dannenmann, another of the five players, pushes forward his entire stock. 'All in,' he says.

Black lifts his sunglasses and studies the board. 'I call.' He matches the huge bet on the table and the players reveal their cards. Black has a pair of nines, which gives him the edge over Dannenmann's pair of sixes and ace high, but there are two more cards to be played. The next card helps nobody. Now only an ace or a six on the last card can beat him. The dealer turns the card … and it's another ace. Black loses the hand and his position is destroyed. A few hours later he finally exits the tournament to a standing ovation from the crowd, who have been captivated by his skill and demeanour. Black has won $1.75 million, but he has lost a tournament that was almost in his grasp, and, visibly upset, he refuses all media interviews.

A few weeks after his Vegas exit, I travelled to Dublin to discover why he has returned to the game he had left behind, and how he squares it with his Dharma practice. What about the manipulative mind games, the lives ruined by gambling, and the focus on winning money and defeating your opponents? What about the sheer, unabashed vulgarity at the end of the tournament, when millions of dollars were emptied onto the table and gleefully clutched by the whooping victor?

Such high-minded criticisms are a sore point for Black. The day before we met, he received a letter from the man who was to have ordained him into the Western Buddhist Order. It said that he couldn't get behind Black's ordination request while he was playing poker. Sitting down to talk in a Dublin restaurant, Black is upset. The 38-year-old is far from the image of reserved, poker-faced cool: his open, expressive face and expansive manner are set off by sharp eyes and a goatee. He opens a book at a quote from the ancient Buddhist scripture describing the lay bodhisattva Vimalakīrti: 'He lived at home, but remained aloof from the realm of desire.... He made his appearance at the fields of sports and in the casinos, but his aim was always to mature those people who were attached to games and gambling.'[*]

Black looks at me with a flash of defiance. 'I used to think, "I can't do that because I am not an enlightened master." But look at the Mahasiddhas. We like to tell stories about these wild, aggressive tantric masters who do crazy things. Well, they're dead! If someone tries to do that today, you get this reaction!'

I haven't come here to judge Black or to determine the ethics of poker; I know that competition poker is a sport, though it connects with a wider world of gambling. I can see its appeal as a contest that demands no athletic prowess and sets people against one another in a battle of minds plus chance. But I am fascinated to know, in the face of Black's protests, how a Dharma practitioner can survive in that world. I can't help but wonder if

---

[*] Robert Thurman (trans.), *The Holy Teaching of Vimalakīrti*, pp.20–1

he is simply succumbing to attachments and encouraging them in others?

Black has had a long journey to get here. Growing up as a Catholic in a Protestant area of Belfast at the height of the Troubles, he had few friends, worked hard, and went to Trinity College, Dublin, to study law. Then he discovered poker. 'I was submerged in poker: I would bring conversations around to it and hone my skills by trying to outwit people in daily interactions.' His early career culminated at the 1997 World Championship, where he got down to the last fourteen and was sitting at the table with Stu 'The Kid' Ungar, reputedly the greatest-ever card player. Ungar lavished Black with attention – and then took his chips. Black had fallen for the oldest trick in the book. He was devastated. Four months later, he made his way to the Dublin Meditation Centre. Initially he hoped that meditation would improve his game, but the teachings he encountered began to resonate on a deeper level for him.

Still haunted by his defeat, Black realized that poker was making him unhappy. 'One day I looked around a poker table and thought, "We're all hungry ghosts"', alluding to the craving-filled beings from Buddhist mythology whose grasping is perpetually frustrated. In 1999, Black moved to the UK to live with other Buddhists from the FWBO and work in Windhorse Trading, a large FWBO-run 'right livelihood' business that offers supportive, shared working conditions for Dharma practitioners. Then he spent two years going door to door asking for regular donations to the Karuna Trust, a charity supporting projects in India that help people considered 'untouchables,' many of whom are now Buddhist converts. Rather than manipulating prospective donors, he found he attracted contributions by being straightforward and making a connection with them.

Black sees this as a training period in which he learned about the Dharma, meditation, and teamwork. But the pull of poker remained. 'I learned a lot about myself, and I was happy to be away from it. But something in me was unmet. Returning to poker, I feel that this is really my life. I'll be honest; I'm obsessed by it, but that obsession brings a lot of focus, which you need in order to excel at anything. If I bring in my spiritual training, I believe this can be a powerful arena for practice.'

Some poker players use math, some use psychology, but Black operates on gut feeling. 'I intensively prepare tactics and analysis before a game, but when I'm playing I just try to be in the present moment. All poker is about making good decisions. I find I make wrong decisions when I act out of tune with my gut sense of how things are: what this person is like, their situation at this moment, and the element of chance. My experience of Buddhist practice means that I also include how I am, how I am treating the other players, and how I respond to both winning and losing. You can disregard that feeling, just like in life, but in poker you get immediate payback. It's always the same lesson: when your actions are not in accordance with how things are, you suffer.'

Losing is one of poker's hard lessons. As well as being highly intelligent, Black is a clearly a very emotional man. 'Because of the element of chance, you can do everything right and still lose. You get hit by unbelievable body blows, which are dictated by statistical probabilities. I work with this by saying, "This will happen."'

I ask what it was like to lose that hand at the World Championship. Black's face creases. 'It was so painful, you have no idea. Afterwards, while I was playing, I was trying to hold the pain without being overwhelmed; to remind myself that what had happened is now the past and I am in the present. Even now, I'll be sitting in meditation turning over the same six or seven hands. *That's* my practice.'

Black saw his return to the tables in summer 2005 as a one-year experiment in combining Dharma practice and poker. But his unexpected success at the World Championships has made this a high-profile adventure. In the years since Black left, the game's popularity has exploded on the Internet and on television, turning it into a multi-billion-dollar industry. His exploits were followed around the world, and in Dublin he's a local celebrity.

One incident that attracted some attention to Black during the World Championships involved his principles. A break in play was called, and when the players returned, one was missing. The announcement of the break had been unclear, and everyone realized that the missing player had simply misunderstood when to return. But the organizers insisted that play recommence and the missing player be eliminated. Incensed, Black protested and tried to enlist the other players' support. They shifted uncomfortably but kept quiet. Black was in tears – visible to the TV audience – as he stalled for time until the player returned.

The incident prompted admiration and discussion about sportsmanship in poker. The game includes bluffing and deception, but does that mean that, within the rules, anything goes? Black believes that ethics still apply, but not simplistically. 'There's a line, and you know when you step over it. You have to look at each case individually, examine your own motivation, and you still need dialogue and communication to help you understand. I assume that, even so, I am still making mistakes and engaging in all sorts of rationalizations, but I think that's a realistic model for trying to act well. It's different from the view that you should withdraw from the world and purify your motivations before engaging.'

Black's Buddhist sensibility clearly comes into play in his response to abusive players. 'Sometimes people try to upset you by being aggressive and insulting. I will say, "There's no need for that." The next stage is to say, "Is this doing you any good?" If there is the slightest element of judgement in me, it doesn't work. I have to connect with the person, and not come from a higher position. I have to genuinely feel, "I'm concerned that this is doing you no good." When I do connect with people in that way, I see their relief that they don't have to be like this.'

Central to Black's plan for maintaining the practice dimension during poker tournaments is sharing the experience with his friend Dōnal Quirke, whom he knows through the FWBO's Dublin centre. 'I want to succeed at poker, but most important is the spiritual journey. I can't do that on my own. I respond to the image of the Buddha's disciples heading off two at a time, connecting intensively with each other and going through things together.' In Vegas, Black and Quirke meditated together in the mornings and sometimes read Dharma texts during breaks in the tournament.

Where Black is an exuberant, commanding personality, Quirke is steady and quiet. He was acting as Black's coach and confidant, discussing the day's play and how his game might improve. He plans to accompany Black on the World Poker Tour that will culminate in the 2006 World Championship. As a man clearly steeped in Dharma practice, what does Quirke make of the world he is entering? 'Vegas is a challenging realm, suffused with ego and greed, and I found those aspects of me were heightened. In the breaks, reading Dharma aloud with Andrew, just hearing the words, 'Thus have I heard,' was like diving into a pool for both of us. I know it had an orienting effect on Andrew as well. But poker's fascinating: coming back from Las Vegas, I was watching it on late-night TV, though of course, you could ask, is anything gained by a group of people sitting around trying to take money off each other?'

I wonder if Quirke thinks Black will be able to sustain his attempt to make poker a practice? His answer is surprising. 'There's my friend Andrew Black, who I've known over the years. But in the poker world there's another person called Andy Black. I think Dharma practice is about not trying to control and manipulate, but that isn't how you win poker tournaments. You need to want to win, and Andy Black is a master of control. But it's complex. Andrew's karma has given him an incredible talent for poker – on his day he's one of the best in the world – but he also has a genuine calling for spiritual practice. I don't think he can just forget Andy Black. He needs to meet this guy, honour him, play the best poker he can, achieve what he can, and then let it go.'

You can't help liking Black, and I found myself envying him – not so much the money or success, but the intensity of his engagement. As he told me, 'One approach to the spiritual life is that you renounce things. Another is to place yourself in the middle of attachments and purify yourself there. We're all imperfect beings struggling along the path, learning as we go. At some point I'll find I've gone as far as I can in the poker world, but at the moment it's incredibly exciting. Let's see how I'm doing in a year.'

_____pilgrimage to auschwitz

Vishvapani

When I announced I was going to do a retreat at Auschwitz, I met many responses. Some people were shocked, as if even uttering 'Auschwitz' was an intrusion or an assault. It is a harsh sound which I, too, soon started to avoid.

A look of pain crossed my father's face when I told him, as if I had touched a wound. 'What good can come of it? What will you do with that experience?' One Buddhist friend asked, 'It is bound to be traumatic, but what is the value of trauma? And what effect will it have on your state of mind?'

Jewish friends said, 'I couldn't go myself. I couldn't bear it.' But others were fascinated by the idea. Many people turned out to have family connections with Jews or Germans and felt fear, guilt, or fascination with the Holocaust. For some, it was a living presence in their lives, as it has been in mine: not a historical event, not a moral conundrum, not a metaphor for personal suffering, but a part of the world, a shadow, a possibility.

When I heard about the retreat, my response was instant: I wanted to go. This was the third retreat at Auschwitz/Birkenau organized by the Zen Peacemakers' Order (ZPO) and led by Roshi Bernie Glassman. I had met Glassman the previous year and liked him. As a Buddhist from a Jewish background I felt intrigued by his freedom in mixing the two traditions. While I have left Judaism behind, I have never stopped feeling a sense of Jewishness – a cultural and historical association rather than a

voices

religious one. My Jewishness seems to manifest whether I like it or not, in the friends I make, my sense of humour, and my way of expressing myself. I have never known what to do with that connection, but in the US a movement has started, inspired by Glassman and others, of Jewish Buddhists exploring their identities. I was also attracted by Glassman's philosophy of 'bearing witness', which means facing the truth, and seeing one's response to it without any desire to fix things. That seemed the right way – the only way – to approach Auschwitz.

Then there was my family connection with the Holocaust. Shortly before leaving I visited my father and we took out the photograph album of his childhood in Berlin. The more questions I asked about Fritz, his father, and Sarah, his grandmother, the quieter he grew. What had happened to Fritz? My father only knew that he had been deported to Minsk in Belarus, and that the letters had stopped. Sarah could have gone to Palestine but she chose to stay, and in the end was deported to the Warsaw ghetto. And then? 'Who knows? She was 70.' My father left Germany in March 1939, aged 10, travelling alone to England under the *kindertransport* scheme. My father's whole life has been shadowed by this experience, but I wonder if those scars have been passed on to me. How have I been affected by this family history, by growing up with the knowledge that the world could contain such cruelty?

In the weeks before the retreat I read some of the extraordinary literature that has grown up around the Holocaust. After reading the accounts by Elie Wiesel or Primo Levi I would dream about concentration camps, as if my mind needed to replay in unconsciousness what it was being told by the books. I felt I was not large enough to contain this truth: the systematic murder of millions of people by dedicated state machinery. I lacked the imagination or the depth to encompass it. Going to a concentration camp was an extension of this encounter, and the retreat, I hoped, would be a chance to 'work it through'.

110

As people gathered at the hotel in Krakow on a clear November day, I saw there would be another dimension to the retreat: the other people, and all the complexities of being with 150 strangers. More than half of those attending were Americans, around the same proportion were Jews, and most were Buddhists, of many denominations and with various overlaps between these groups.

On the first evening a bunch of us visited a restaurant in Kazimiertz, the old Jewish quarter, and I talked to Jinny. Her father had been in Auschwitz, but he had never spoken about it, and he exerted a tyrannical discipline over the family. When he did mention the camps it was as a basis for emotional blackmail. 'Why do you need new shoes? When I was in the camps we would have done anything for shoes like you are throwing away!' Now she runs an organization that brings together the children of survivors and of ss officers. In her terms I qualified, as she called my father 'a survivor'. I'd never thought of him that way.

Over the next few days I met many people with similar stories. There was Eva, who had left on the *kindertransport*, like my father, but she had travelled on to the US where she had become a literature professor. She was now finding the courage to explore the fate of the family she left behind. Early on I made friends with Rod, a Theravādin Buddhist from Manchester, and also Jewish – a kind, quiet man who felt drawn to attend but confused about his reasons for doing so. I also got to know Nancy Baker, a philosopher and Zen teacher from New York, who spoke of her near-death experience as a child, after she was thrown through a car window. She has worked with dying people for many years and coming to Auschwitz was a further encounter with death.

Many of those on the retreat were from Zen groups connected with Maezumi Roshi, Bernie Glassman's teacher, and some came each year. Soon I felt like a stranger at a class reunion, a party where everyone knew everyone except for me. In the restaurant Jinny was talking to Heinz, a German Zen teacher, and they swapped tales about last year's retreat. 'It's funny to see you looking happy and relaxed in a restaurant,' she said. 'For five days last year you looked like you wanted to commit suicide!'

On the first day of the retreat we visited the Jewish areas of Krakow. A guide described how the Nazis had gradually increased the restrictions on the Jews. After the laws banning them from working came the yellow stars, and then transfers to the ghetto, where a few streets housed 15,000 people in incredible squalor. Finally the ghetto was cleared and they were deported to Auschwitz. At every stage the inhabitants retained a vestige of optimism, and even believed the Germans when they were told that they were being sent to a new life in the Ukraine. Things seemed so bad that people thought they could not get worse. Few had the courage or the insight to realize just how bad they could be.

The sense of being trapped by a vast, insuperable power was my overwhelming impression from the Holocaust accounts I had read. On my first day in Poland I read *Fragments* by Binjamin Wilkomirski, an evocation of childhood memories of the camps, which gave me fresh nightmares. After the war Wilkomirski believed the outside world was, in fact, the camp – but disguised. It is a peculiar, infectious mentality, and on the journey to Oswicien (the town the Germans renamed Auschwitz) I found myself jumping at words like 'transport' and 'Reichsbaum'. It was as if all the hidden, mysterious forces that make the world function, and on which we depend without awareness or comprehension, were turned hostile and malevolent. Later I read that Wilkomirski's memories were most likely fantasies, and he had never been in a camp at all. But the book retained its hallucinatory effect. The bus travelled on through a thick fog, past increasingly bleak landscapes, weather-fended buildings, and straggly pine forest. I dozed most of the way, then woke with a jolt and a rush of anxiety, the severe brick buildings looming outside the window: 'This is Auschwitz.'

We were assigned rooms in a flurry of confusion and then assembled in small groups. Frank Ostaseski, the group leader, established an atmosphere of openness and warmth. 'Speak from the heart', he said, 'speak spontaneously.' He is an impressive man who founded a Buddhist hospice in San Francisco. Each morning at 7 a.m. we met as a group to share our experiences. When my turn came I was moved, even choked, speaking of my family and my motivations for coming.

The next day we toured Auschwitz and Birkenau. Auschwitz was the original camp, housed in a converted Austrian barracks, and now maintained as a museum. The displays have the artificiality of any museum, but still they overwhelmed me with a mass of impressions. Spectacles taken from the dead, like a huge pile of insects; human hair in an incredible quantity, all the same colour – shocked white by age, fear, and chemicals; a standing cell in the punishment block where four people were squashed together, upright for days on end; the famous sign 'Arbeit Macht Frei'.

We gathered at the Execution Wall. The square in front of the wall is a place of unutterable bleakness, surrounded by sheer walls, their windows blanked out – a prison inside a prison. One woman buckled at the knees, tears streaming down her face; and Rabbi Don Singer led Kaddish, the Jewish prayer for the dead. At first I bridled at this, with my old resistance to Judaism, but as the singing continued I realized, to my surprise, that I knew the words and I joined in, moved by their melancholy beauty.

Birkenau was the concentration camp of my imagination, the one I had been dreaming about for weeks, the one I had pictured from films, documentaries, and photographs. When the Nazis decided on the Final Solution of the 'Jewish problem' in 1942 they chose Oswicien as its centrepiece, and two miles from the original camp they constructed Birkenau. It was both a work camp and a death camp. While Auschwitz housed 20,000, Birkenau eventually contained three times that number.

Rows of barracks stretched beyond the barbed-wire fence, and the railway tracks lengthened between them. I was unprepared for the vastness of Birkenau, or the desolation this brought; for the camp's oppressive orderliness, the barbarous symmetry, the hideous symbolism of the rails leading through the camp to the gas chambers, the barbed wire taut and implacable, the wretchedness of the barracks. Yet the occupants were the lucky ones, saved from immediate extermination to form a vast slave army and worked to death for the sake of the German economy.

As I walked beside the tracks I recalled the pictures and books I had read, and tried to open myself to what had happened here. This is where the trains stopped and the selections took place – right for labour, left for death. This is where they walked, the condemned, thinking they had been chosen for light work. And this is where they died, where the tracks end at the gas chambers, which now lie in ruins. One and a half million people, in an endless stream. A huge factory of death. But even standing on the very spot of their murder, I could not encompass such suffering. People around me cried severally, each sparked by a specific detail – or a different point in the accumulation of details. By the end of the afternoon I felt numb.

In the evening we met as one large group and Eve Marko of the zpo stood in for Bernie Glassman, who had not arrived. She spoke movingly about the Peacemaker precepts. The first is 'Not Knowing': staying open to the reality of the situation, free from preconceptions. She said we all had a question in coming here, whether that was, 'How could people do this to other people?' or 'Why did this happen?'

'Stay with that question,' she said, 'and don't try to answer it too quickly. That question is also the question of your life, the mystery at the heart of you.'

It had been a long day, and Eve was exhausted. She asked Rabbi Singer to sing from the Psalms. Then, in an ecumenical gesture, he asked two Christian nuns to join him. They seemed rather on show, so they got some others to stand up. Then someone said, 'Come on! Everybody join in!' and suddenly the whole mass of people was on its feet, dancing in a huge circle around the auditorium. I left. It wasn't possible to stay without joining in, and others left, too. Only Rod stayed sitting in the middle, crying quietly and oblivious to what was happening. Eva came out in tears. 'I joined in because everyone else was having such a good time and I didn't want to spoil it.' I had read before arriving how in past years a sense of celebration had mysteriously emerged from the contemplation of the darkness of Auschwitz. Now the participants seemed to be trying to recreate that experience on the first evening. It felt like an evasion, a bid for transcendence that became a descent into schmaltz.

The next day we set up our meditation cushions in a ring around the tracks at Birkenau, which was the focus for the next three days. We sat in a circle, buttressed against the Polish winter by layers of clothing. Some of the time – not enough for me – we just sat quietly, absorbing the atmosphere. Each day we chanted the names of people who had died from a book that lists 60,000, a mere fraction of the victims. But the names helped to personalize the statistics: 'Stephan Kulczyk, Joseph Kulda, Wladislaw Kulejwski.' Each one seemed for a moment to stand before us. Sometimes the same name was read again and again: 'Max Cohen, Max Cohen, Max Cohen.'

One day as we recited names I heard, 'Bloom, Bloom, Bloomberg, Bloomenbaum.' My heart skipped a beat as the reader approached my family's name: 'Blumenfeldt, Blumenfeldt.' I could not make out the first names. Could Fritz have been there?

When the readings ended I jumped up to find the reader. She had gone, but I explained what I wanted to the people who had been next to her. My knees weakened and tears came.

Later I wandered through the camp sitting in the ruins of huts, in the barracks, by the gas chambers. The buildings have hardly changed, and the former inhabitants seemed close by. Birkenau is an awesome product of massive energy and powerful intelligence, testimony to the human capacity for methodical, premeditated sadism. Forgiveness seemed a distant idea – premature, even impertinent. How could I forgive on behalf of the dead? In any case, what I felt was not hatred as much as sadness and bewilderment.

Each of us, it seemed, was struggling to make sense of our experience. One Jewish man described asking a German on the retreat if he could imagine having been a guard. The German replied that he could well imagine that.

'So if we were both back there. I think you would have shot me.'

'Most probably, yes.'

Another wondered how he would have acted if he had been in the camp. 'Would I have been a *kapo* (a prisoner organizing camp affairs for the Germans)? Would I have learned how to survive?'

Another Jewish man described walking through Auschwitz with two non-Jewish friends thinking, 'If this was back then, you'd be all right, and he'd be all right, but I'd be in deep shit!' We are all troubled by the ignorance of the people who went to the gas chambers thinking they were taking a shower. 'Why didn't someone yell, "You are going to your deaths!"?'

Auschwitz was a spiritual test. People talked about the moral issues it raised, or what it told them about human nature. But for me, asking, 'How could people do this?' seemed an abstraction. I wanted simply to witness the suffering that had taken place in the camp. Sometimes, as I sat, I was confronted with images of that pain, and felt a raw, visceral sympathy. I wanted to stay with that rawness, without evading or interpreting it. But my mind would slip off into its usual preoccupations, or be attracted or irritated by others on the retreat.

When a German man said to me, 'Being here reminds me that I have a concentration camp inside myself,' I felt insulted, even angry.

'He may have some emotional blocks,' I thought, 'But how can you equate the two? Is Auschwitz for him just a psychological metaphor?'

The next day I expressed my frustrations to my group. 'I feel critical of the ways we make sense of our experience: of the tendency to psychologize, as if the significance of Auschwitz is that it puts you in touch with your personal griefs; or to dramatize, making stories out of our responses, with moments of pathos and irony to provide appropriate light and shade; and of the desire to move beyond horror into love and joy. I just want to stay with the reality of what happened. But I can't, it keeps slipping away, I can't maintain that state for long.'

Frank said, 'Be mindful in all of your actions. If you are walking, walk more slowly – halve the pace. And have a sense of continuity, the flow of experience. Savour each moment in the short time we have here.'

Meditating in the grounds I experimented with different practices. Before leaving Britain I had taken up the Vajrasattva practice, invoking a Buddha whose healing radiance blesses and purifies all beings. The mantra of Vajrasattva is a potent invocation, but at Birkenau the sounds seemed empty. I reverted to simpler practices – radiating love, or just sitting with my experience. Sometimes in meditation I had a sense of a vast, brooding, unquiet spirit, or a distant moan. I saw images of writhing bodies. One day as I meditated I felt that roots might grow down from my body, deep into the earth, and that I could not be overwhelmed by Birkenau's horror. That evening I was filled with exhilaration and energy. Spending my time meditating and reflecting, seeking to understand myself, and to gain a sympathetic understanding of others, I was doing what I most want to do with my life. Tantric yogis in India would live in cremation grounds, surrounded by the remnants of corpses and the spirits of the dead, and there they would confront their deepest fears. Birkenau is a modern cremation ground in the most literal sense.

As the retreat drew to an end, I spoke to others about their experience. Nancy Baker told me it had helped her to resolve issues she had been struggling with for years. 'I felt I came into contact with a bottomless well of tears, and I was overwhelmed by a compassionate weeping, without knowing why. This seemed to wash me clean of whatever aversion I have to death. I feel I have come away as a bigger container for suffering.'

Frank Ostaseski drew on his hospice experience. 'In my work I look at death and I believe that to be fully alive means to be prepared to see death. It is the same with evil. I don't believe in the "Hitler within", but I can be cruel and critical, and left unchecked these tendencies could lead to evil. One way of bringing awareness to that is to look at evil outside – it helps us to see what is good and whole and makes us face ourselves very frankly. This is a raw place, and it needs to be kept raw, not tidied up or made comfortable. There are places of great inspiration in the world, but here we see the wound, and that helps to make us more whole.'

The most moving part of each day for me was reciting the Kaddish. It seemed to possess a profound resonance that the Sanskrit chants lacked here. Standing by the gas chambers, we chanted in Hebrew, and read the verses in many languages. The words of the Kaddish continued to echo when I returned to Britain. 'Oseh shalom bim'romav, hu ya'se shalom, alenu v'alkol

Yisrael, v'imru amen.' (The one who has given a universe of peace gives peace to us, to all that is Israel, to all humanity. And say, yes. Amen.) We lit candles for the dead. 'Fourteen thousand a day,' Rabbi Singer said. 'A vast stream of humanity, men, women, and children, all jostled together. And they knew. Some at least knew what was happening. "What's that coming out of the chimney", one woman asked. "That's us," came the reply.'

Bernie Glassman arrived late, coming straight from a solitary retreat he had been on for the seven months since his wife's death. He did not take a lead, but when he spoke on the retreat's penultimate night he drew many strands together. He quoted the advice of his friend, the Jewish cabbala teacher Zalman Schachter, about the retreat: 'Go for the souls, not for your own transformation.' That crystallized what I wanted to do myself: to remember and to grieve. Primo Levi writes that the ss guards taunted the prisoners by saying that not only would they be killed, but that all evidence of their fates would be obliterated as well. And, if by some chance, word of the camps got out, it would not be believed. That threat of oblivion was the worst humiliation. One thing I could do was bear witness to the Holocaust through my silent vigil.

giving it large

Peter Cogger

'Get up, you little shit. Don't you know how much I've got riding on this!' The unmistakable voice, through gritted teeth, of my father, over the noise of the crowd going wild. My father used to ridicule any man who wouldn't put up his son to fight me for a wager in the back rooms of rough London pubs. Hot goods were exchanged for hard cash and illegal gambling thrived. This was where I learned to fight. Other fathers were so much drunker that matches were easily set up. This time a boy had been brought in from Tottenham, north-east London. His dad was laughing, holding up a blue £5 note. The boy, about 12, was 18 inches taller than me and had arms that seemed longer than my mother's. I was only 8 years old. It was a set-up. He had a grey vest with the name of a boxing club on it. He wore boots with black rubber caps over the inside ankles that I had never seen before, and started prancing and dancing when he caught me looking at them. My only reassurance was that he was wearing boxing gloves, which I knew were nice and soft.

Money started changing hands fast. I felt sick. There was shouting, pushing, scraping back of tables. And then whack, whack! It had started, and already I couldn't breathe through my nose. Then I was sitting on my arse, legs straight out in front of me. But when he kicked me I remembered how my mother had kicked me – she would beat me after being hit by my father, yelling, 'You're just like him,' and I felt really angry for the first time in my life.

I was going in for the kill when my father came and held my arms down. 'Enough, enough.' It went very quiet for a moment and then wild – and an almighty punch-up started as bets were paid out. I got a cash bonus and another cider, which was considered a soft drink in the 1960s. In this way, at the age of 7 or 8, I could earn seventeen shillings in a weekend (about one-fifth of an adult's weekly wage).

My family was poor and Dad would often turn to crime rather than work harder. One night, when I was 5, I was woken up in the night. My father had taken delivery of a lorry load of stolen shoes, and three men were lugging them upstairs into my bedroom. They took out the mattress but lost patience when it wouldn't fit back in again, so they wedged it, folded double between the empty fireplace and the floor-to-ceiling boxes. I stood there in my itchy tartan dressing-gown. If I went down and complained I would be screamed at, hit, and promptly sent back up, so I tried to curl up in its hollow. It was bitterly cold by the chimney and eventually I sneaked into my sisters' room. I twisted the door handle very slowly and lifted the edge of the covers just enough to slide in a leg, then my tummy. It was no use. One of my elder sisters whacked, then kicked. I hit the lino floor with a hard thump to my hip and head. Never again, I vowed, as I lay coldly on that very spot until dawn.

So that was my background. It was a hard upbringing, which has had a strong influence. My best friend often said, 'It would have been so easy for you to have become a crook.' But instead I've ended up as a Buddhist. In some mysterious way these experiences have made me what I am.

When I was 11, my dad must have pulled off a big job, because suddenly we became much better off, and I was sent to a posh boarding school. I felt different from the other children there, who came from wealthy families. I craved stability and love. Always in the back of my mind was the fact that other dads from my own background disappeared (into prison). I thought money would bring the stability I longed for. I wanted to show the rich kids that I could make more than them. And I wanted to show my father I could do it legally. I decided I was going to make a million pounds. It really wasn't as big a deal as people made out. I knew it was quite possible for anyone with enough bottle. It just involved hard work, common sense, and keeping your eyes open.

I left school at 16 and was soon running my own restaurant. I realized that to be successful in business all you had to do was find out what people want and sell it to them. Before long I had everything anyone could wish for: £1,000 suits, handmade shirts, seventeen houses, five cars, exotic holidays. I could buy a house on Friday and by Monday forget I'd bought it. I remember my bank manager taking me to lunch and saying, 'There's nothing you couldn't buy.'

At the same time I was becoming dependent on alcohol and cocaine. An outside fix for an inside problem. My search for oblivion through drink had started early – at the age of 12 I was in the school sickbay for three days with alcohol poisoning. But when you have pocketfuls of money it's hard to believe people when they say, 'Booze is destroying your life.' My idea of success was material. I never guessed that I'd soon voluntarily give up this wealth that had represented so much to me, and actively embrace a life of increasing simplicity. When I was 31 I decided to seek help for my drinking, and I met people who were happy – not because of money but because of their spiritual path. But it took several more years to realize that quality of life has nothing to do with standard of living.

When I started eating at the Wild Cherry restaurant in East London, I was at a really low ebb. I didn't know why I was drawn there – it certainly wasn't the vegetarian food, nor the fact that I had to queue for lunch. Then one morning I met Sandra Greenway, one of the staff, in the street. It was a significant day. I was about to go to court and lie, to avoid serious motoring charges. As part of my programme to stop drinking, I would usually pray every day. That morning, knowing what I was about to do, I hadn't been able to pray. It would have been like trying to bargain with God.

I found myself asking Sandra, 'Why are you lot so nice?'

'We're Buddhists,' was her simple reply.

Suddenly I realized the motley collection of women who served my lunch, and seemed genuinely to care how I was, were working together for a common purpose – that touched me deeply.

Sandra was saying, 'We're a Buddhist team, working together because of our shared ideals.'

My inner response was, 'And I'm a little shit who's got everything, but nothing.'

She didn't need to say anything else. It highlighted that I was about to disgrace everything I believed in, and defy everything I thought was decent … because it suited me.

I realized I might as well be dead as go into court, swear on my honour, then lie. But I was in a terrible dilemma. If I told the truth I could go to prison. In the end I went early and asked the Crown Prosecution to change my eleven pleas to guilty. I told the coordinator the whole story. She was astonished that someone would admit to telling lies. Then she astonished me by throwing out all but part of one charge.

Suddenly everything in my life changed. It was like I threw in the towel and stopped fighting. I realized we have a choice in every moment of our lives. I learned Buddhist meditation at the London Buddhist Centre and I went on retreat. One of my main practices now is *dāna* (generosity). Buddhism has taught me to look at greed. I used to spend an extra £100 on food for my fridge each week, just so that I had more choice, and then routinely throw it away without a thought.

My pride and joy was a gleaming black 911 Carrera Sport, fitted with every extra, and the last of the handmade Porsches. One Buddhist friend remarked, 'You don't drive as quickly as you did before you started meditating, Peter. Do you still need to hurry?'

'No, not these days, since cutting the work back,' I replied.

'Is the car a good investment then?' she enquired.

'Not really,' I replied.

'Oh I see, you must need to impress your clients, be seen to be successful,' she said.

'Not at all, I hardly ever see them any more.' I slowly replied. The seed was sown. Why did I need a 170mph car in London, or anywhere for that matter? I sold it before noon the next day and took a biscuit tin to carry the £25,000 cash.

I rang to tell my somewhat-shocked friend and added, 'I've never felt so free in my life.' I didn't know what to do with the money. To reinvest it would keep me bound up with the very things I was trying to be free of. So at first I did nothing. The biscuit tin sat in my kitchen for several months. When I needed a lesson, I would go and look in it. I nearly burned it a few times. Then I bought the Dāna Car – a loan car available for those in the local Buddhist community who cannot afford their own car. I think of generosity in terms of sharing what you have, responding to what people need, rather than just 'giving'.

Not all giving is generosity. It can be buying yourself out of trouble, a kind of guilt avoidance. As a kid I would often only do good things when there was a pay-off. Later I carried a chip on my shoulder. I would lend someone something and if they didn't say thank you, I'd feel like running after them saying, 'Don't you realize what a big thing it is for me to give that away?'

I've also had to learn to be appropriate in giving. I used to be like a comedy character from British 1980s TV called Loadsamoney, a parody of working-class traders who made it rich in the Thatcher era. I remember seeing a couple of Buddhist friends in a café. I went up to them and tried to buy them cake to go with their coffee. Even when they refused I still insisted – didn't they even want a biscuit? They grew quite exasperated and eventually I realized they didn't want anything. Now I see that to be generous includes being sensitive to the other person. What I thought was generosity was born of insecurity, my need to be approved of and liked.

I believe that any material thing doesn't attain its true value until it is a gift. For me, the art of generosity is to keep looking for opportunities to give. I tend to choose things that are not obvious, that perhaps would not otherwise get support. A big part of my giving is to remain anonymous. I call myself a dāna sniper. In the supermarket I keep a look-out for people who are obviously short of cash, usually pensioners. I would never insult their dignity by offering them money, my trick is to fold up a note and drop it by their feet. I point it out to them, and often they say it isn't theirs. 'Don't you want it then?' I ask. Now they hesitate. 'Can I?' I get such delight in handing it to them, much more pleasure than I would have in spending the money myself. It's thrilling, although I got caught out when I approached the same lady twice.

As well as giving up much material wealth through choice, being cheated by a former business partner means that I may be forced to give up even more, including my home. But I haven't lost sleep over this. A few years ago I'd never have dreamed I could respond so calmly. One old friend thought he had a much better solution for the person who has been causing me trouble. 'Why don't you get him removed?' he suggested. 'Permanently.' That was the world I used to inhabit.

But now, as I opened the most recent solicitor's letter, I smiled. I smiled because now I know that real contentment comes from not hanging on to things. I know that no one can take away my friendships. No one can make me drink again. No one can take away the Dharma.

PART TWO:*reflections*

_____*from black panthers to lions*

Jan Willis
profiled by Suryagupta

'"Don't go too far!" my mother always reminded me as she pushed open the screen door and I rocketed forth, straight past her.' In Alabama these words were more than ordinary motherly advice. They contained a warning: Don't cross the line, the rigid racial boundaries that ran through the mining village of Docena, Alabama. For a black child growing up in the racially segregated South, the consequences of not adhering to the geographical and social limits were severe. 'Every so often, Docena's Ku Klux Klan reminded us blacks of our "proper" place. Their tactics were simple: they reminded us of who was boss by instilling in us fear of the consequences of ever forgetting it. None of the blacks who lived in Docena was spared the Klan's reminders. On a fairly regular basis, there were drive-throughs and cross-burnings in the Camp.'

This is the background to the early chapters of *Dreaming Me*, Jan Willis's autobiography, which also describes her involvement with the civil rights movement, her travels to India, and her relationship with Lama Thubten Yeshe. Coming to terms with her true self has involved making peace with her turbulent growing up in the South.

Even a trip in the family car warranted the warning not to wind down the window for fear of Klan members throwing acid at them. The threat of violence at the hands of the Klan was ever present for Willis and her family. On one occasion she woke to find Klansmen, women and children – her neighbours – burning

131

a cross on her front lawn. 'The minutes stretched into eternity as we waited for a bomb. But, cross ablaze and garbled speeches delivered, the Klansmen and women and their enrobed children got back into their cars and rode away. For whatever reason that night our lives were spared.'

The psychological effect of such experiences was crushing, and it would take years of Buddhist meditation under the skilful guidance of Lama Yeshe before Willis could directly engage with a process of transformation and healing. Yet somehow, despite the oppressive conditions, she was able to see and think beyond the limitations imposed by segregation. Her keen intellect was noted by family and teachers, and this brought both encouragement and trepidation since no one in Docena dared to dream big dreams for a black girl, for whom the world might prove an unkind place. But Willis was compelled to go beyond her mother's advice not to venture too far, and she was one of only four pupils in her year to go to college, and the only one to attend one of the prestigious Ivy League universities in the North.

Fortunately there was more to life in Docena than the Klan, as the small mining village contained a source of religious inspiration. Although Willis had to be cajoled into being baptized, that baptism became her first spiritual experience. 'It was as though my family became infinitely larger. I had joined a new community and there was strength and grace there.'

Willis now embraces her Baptist roots by calling herself an African-American Baptist Buddhist, and she sees no contradiction. 'It's the most honest description I can give of myself,' she says. 'When I'm working through some important issue, I turn to Buddhist principles, but when times are really dire I call on both.' In *Dreaming Me*, Willis recounts the story of a plane journey to illustrate the point.

> The plane veered steeply upwards.... We were like astro-nauts, our heads pressed back against our seats, our

bodies feeling the G-forces of lift-off.... I started to pray, at first aloud and then silently, but speeded up, with urgency.... 'Lama Yeshe,' I screamed, 'May I never be separated from you in this or future lives!' Gripping my armrests in silence, I continued, 'May you and all the Buddhas help and bless us now!' Without pausing, I then fervently intoned, 'Christ Jesus, please help us. Please, I pray, bless me and all these people!'[*]

She goes on to quote Kirkegaard's dictum, 'One doesn't know what one really believes until one is forced to act.'

In the late sixties the United States was in the grip of social and political upheaval. The Vietnam war was stirring young and thoughtful Americans to protest. Martin Luther King, who had led the peaceful movement for social justice, had been assassinated. The new word on many lips was 'revolution'. Black radicals felt the need for a more assertive strategy to fight injustice, feeling that, despite years of peaceful demonstrations and sacrifice on the part of black activists, nothing fundamental had changed. The Black Panthers emerged, taking 'a more aggressive stance' and prepared to use violence if necessary. Equal rights had still to be achieved. This meant they would no longer try to raise the conscience of America by enduring the violent opposition to peaceful demands for justice, but would advocate 'self defence'. For the first time the fight for equal rights took on a military stance.

This threw Willis into turmoil. Like many of her contemporaries she had already discovered Buddhism through the works of Alan Watts and D.T. Suzuki. The images of Vietnamese monks and nuns protesting against the war and persecution of their religion by setting fire to themselves while meditating and chanting had impressed her deeply. Transformation through nonviolent means strongly appealed, yet her experience had not proved that the way of peace worked. Even though she was now

[*] Jan Willis, *Dreaming Me*, Riverhead Books, p.310

at the elite Cornell University she still felt the impact of racism. She found good friends, but she felt the hostility and hypocrisy of their parents. One night a cross was burned on the lawn outside a black women's residence.

Willis first went to India in her junior year at Cornell, studying Buddhist philosophy at a summer school. While visiting a Buddhist festival she met a monk who told her she should study at the monastery and she corresponded with the monk even after her return to Cornell. In her senior year one of her professors asked what she planned to do after graduation. A choice presented itself: armed struggle and revolution with people she knew and respected in the Black Panthers, or the way of peace in a Tibetan monastery. She hadn't thought through the implications of violence but, she told me, 'I saw that nonviolence hadn't worked and thought there must be another way. In the end I felt too afraid and too confused to take up guns. Besides, I'd always preferred peace and nonviolent methods.' Willis's professors made her a unique offer: she would be admitted to graduate studies at Cornell and granted her first year there *in absentia*, which meant she could return to the monastery at Cornell's expense. 'When I finally decided to study at the monastery, a huge weight fell from my shoulders.'

When she first met Lama Yeshe, Willis was impressed by his smile, his gentleness, and his intelligence and quickness of mind. 'He understood me in ways I didn't understand myself.' Studying Tibetan Buddhism with more than sixty monks, and engaging in visualization practices, Willis discovered the tools she needed to free herself from confusion and anger. Meeting Lama Yeshe and the community of Tibetan exiles provided her with essential support. 'Tibetans are a wonderfully joyous and gentle people who have managed to cope with a historical trauma in some ways similar to black folks. They took me in right away and for that I'm grateful.' Some time later she discovered her vocation teaching Buddhism at university level and translating Tibetan texts.

Willis emphasizes that her transformation is still under way and the journey to freedom is by no means complete. However, she has found a continual source of inspiration and peace through the Dharma and Lama Yeshe.

When she first encountered Buddhism, Willis was outwardly strong and confident – a high achiever. But she now thinks that this proud exterior masked 'a lifetime's worth of self-pity and low self-esteem'. It took her ten years of Buddhist practice before she could confront the racial dimension of this insecurity and put aside her anger. Of one meeting with Lama Yeshe she says,

> It was as if Lama Yeshe were saying, 'Let the old wounds go, daughter. Let them all go.' Standing there with him, for the first time in my life I began to feel that I could let them go; let them all go and embrace my true self, which was, like the true selves of all other beings, clear, confident, capable, loving, and lovable. At that moment, confidence arose strongly in me, and I knew that everyone ought to feel this way.*

Tibetan tantric practices, such as reflecting on one's essential inner purity, or visualizing oneself as a Buddha, were also helpful. In time Willis saw the inner causes of her discontent, as well as the outer, social causes.

> Whether our suffering takes the guise of self-pity or self-absorption, its source is the same: holding too tightly to our projected images of ourselves. We know, for example, that when we are depressed, our minds turn about one point: me. Poor me. Why me? How could this have happened to me? The nub is always me, me, me....†

*ibid. p.300
†ibid. p.167

Through her years of practice Willis has come to embody the Dharma name given to her in 1969 by Geshe Rabten, Lama Yeshe's teacher, which translates as 'Joy of the Dharma'. She is now well known for the passion, clarity, and humour with which she communicates both the letter and spirit of Buddhism.

There have been three decades of equal rights for African-Americans, and affirmative action programmes have attempted to redress the social and political imbalances caused by the history of slavery and racism. Yet when I asked if racism still has a strong effect on American society, Willis did not hesitate. 'Absolutely and unquestionably. An excellent example was the recent travesty with our presidential elections and the disqualified or uncounted votes in Florida.' The majority of these votes were cast by black people, which brought questions for people who had fought for civil rights over many years and believed they had been successful.

According to Willis, 'mainstream Buddhist groups consist of mainly white "elite" Buddhists, and that reflects the divide in society.' In fact there are very few African-American Buddhists, and mainstream Buddhist groups are often not successful in maintaining the interest and commitment of blacks. Willis argues that both blacks and whites come to Buddhist practice with a great deal of racial conditioning. Whites have imbibed often negative messages and views about blacks and their position in society from history books, popular culture, and from family and friends. Blacks' memories of the struggle for legal and political rights and the history of racial subjugation means that they enter a mainly white context, such as a Dharma centre, with trepidation. So even in the calm and positive environment of a Buddhist centre, racial history and experiences of racism will be present. 'I don't think there is any reason to think that our sanghas are so different from the larger societies in which we live. Prejudice exists there as it does in society, even if there is an attempt to do better,' says Willis.

Willis would like to see more cultural and ethnic diversity within Buddhist groups, so she is raising awareness of racial issues in Buddhist communities. She sees this as a way for both black and white Buddhists to free themselves from negative conditioning. Her approach is to address the issues using tools with which Buddhists are familiar. 'I think we need to use what we know how to do best, namely meditation.'

Meditative awareness can be brought to the subject of race: 'We need to develop contemplative exercises geared to developing awareness of race and transforming negative judgements into positive ones.' Willis uses the Gelug school of Tibetan Buddhism's technique of contemplating teachings and ideas, and she introduces these into workshops on race. These workshops explore how we relate to difference, and introduce Buddhist values and principles, such as loving-kindness. She cautions, however, that before engaging in these activities it is important to have a 'safe space' where there is a degree of trust and openness: 'The subject of race raises a lot of intense and difficult emotions.' Whites tend to feel guilty or defensive when the subject is brought up, while blacks often resent having to educate others about their experience and history. She is confident, though, that addressing the issue directly can bring deeper harmony and understanding.

Willis draws inspiration from her first meeting with the Dalai Lama during a student protest at the height of America's civil unrest. He advocated patience, clarity, and loving-kindness when faced with difficult situations. For Willis these are the same qualities needed to explore differences based on race or culture. 'We need the imaginative exchange of self and other ... placing oneself in another person's shoes and recognizing the preciousness of another human being.' For Willis this is the meaning of the title 'religious innovator' she was given by *Time* magazine. 'I think teaching and raising awareness about the racial divide and trying to fashion mediations to help transform negative judgements about others and oneself is worth doing. I'm trying to contribute what I can to that endeavour.'

In *Dreaming Me,* Willis describes a series of dreams featuring lionesses that occurred while she was tracing her family history.

> The lions invaded my dreams and my pysche.... The lions are me, myself. Perhaps they are my deepest African self. They are the 'me' that I have battled ever since ... venturing forth into a mostly white world. I believe it is time to let the lions come to the fore and to make peace with them. For making peace with them is making peace with myself, allowing me to be me, authentically.[*]

To meet Willis is to see this lioness quality.

---

[*] ibid. p.317

_transforming terror

Christopher Titmuss
interviewed by Vishvapani

Christopher greeted me at his house in Totnes, south-west England, in a large black hat, long black raincoat, and trailing black scarf. A senior teacher in the Insight Meditation movement, Titmuss is without the cool reserve of some of his contemporaries. In Buddhist circles he has dispensed with his surname and now prefers to be known simply as Christopher. He has large, friendly eyes and an immediately engaging manner. Engagement is one of his themes. 'I recently told one Dharma group, "I think I prefer Muslims to Buddhists. At least they have some fire, some passion...." It was a provocative way of saying that I think Buddhists can be so "nice", and so passive.'

We met to discuss a book Christopher published in 2002, in the wake of the terrorist attacks of September 11th, called _Transforming our Terror: a spiritual approach to making sense of senseless tragedy_. 'I have been visiting the US for twenty-five years, but mainly to lead retreats. So the America I encounter is the American mind. I noticed that after 9/11 there was a great deal more fear and anxiety among the people I was teaching. I started to ask myself, what can Buddhist practice say to this experience?'

The result is an inquiry into the nature of fear, grief, loss, and how the human mind processes and makes sense of them. In essence, Christopher suggests, the collective emotional response to the public trauma of the terrorist attacks mirrored the patterns of personal responses to grief that, in his book, he describes so well.

The sadness that permeates our hearts due to the arising of the unwelcome, the unwanted, and the unforeseen has a certain weight that can bear down on us until we feel sick to our stomachs. Our chests contract and our heads feel stuffed full of unpleasant sensations. The overall pressure releases tears out of our eyes as the breathtakingly painful information begins to sink deeper and deeper into our hearts.*

Implicit in the analogy between how an individual responds to suffering and how a community responds to a collective tragedy is a critique of the War on Terror that America launched in response to 9/11.

'They decided that the way to combat their fear was to hit out. But that involves narrowing down imaginatively, cutting off from the suffering of the other person. In my book I have stories about the suffering of people in Palestine and Afghanistan, but when I submitted the manuscript, the US publisher wanted me to cut these out. Essentially they said, "Can you keep it just to the experience of Americans?" But I replied, "What I am writing about is universal. The Dharma doesn't distinguish between Americans or Afghanis. All it knows about is human beings – their minds and their suffering." Eventually, when I gave an ultimatum, "Publish everything or nothing," they backed down and it was printed. But this was an insight into the atmosphere in America after 9/11 and the unconscious forces of censorship that have taken hold.'

I was struck by the eloquence of Christopher's descriptions of grief and sadness, and I asked if they grew from his own experiences. Surprisingly, he answered in the negative. 'I seem to be blessed with a happy, equanimous inner life, and of course I have put in many years of hard-core Dharma practice. I can't remember the last time I found something hard to bear, or I suffered.' Christopher spent six years in the 1970s as a Theravādin

---

* *Transforming our Terror*, p.18

Buddhist monk in Thailand, where he studied vipassanā meditation under Ajahn Dhammadharo and essence of Dharma under Ajahn Buddhadasa, and in India. Since then he has been based at Gaia House in Devon and has taught meditation in centres around the world. As well as this he has been an energetic activist, mediating in conflict situations and working as an active campaigner for peaceful solutions.

Christopher's assertion that he experiences little or no suffering is all the more striking as his life has not been without difficulty. He was recently suspended as a teacher by Gaia House and another leading insight meditation retreat centre, following an allegation by a female student that he 'pursued her and avoided her' during a weekend retreat.

He commented, 'I believe in the intimacy of offering whole-hearted attention to a person rather than becoming a detached professional. I regard this as the essence of being a kalyāṇa mitra [good spiritual friend] to others. We have to take the risk that we will be misunderstood and accept the consequences.'

Rather than through his own personal suffering, Christopher suggests that his encounter with the painful emotions he describes has come principally through listening to the experience of others. 'I learn so much through listening to the grief, sorrow, and terror of people I work with. I practise the art of witnessing their experience, just as in meditation you witness the thoughts and feelings that arise, while neither becoming lost in them nor cutting off from them.'

Instead of responding to pain and loss with anger or dejection, Buddhist psychology suggests that awareness is the key to a more creative response. Christopher returns repeatedly to this theme of witnessing, evoking the biblical resonances of 'bearing witness'. In *Transforming our Terror* he writes, 'The true witness is not passive, but tries to take an overview and maintains a sense of caring responsibility for the totality of the event, free

141

from bias.' In some accounts such awareness can seem cool and detached, but Christopher emphasizes sensitivity to experience and – that dangerous word again – 'intimacy' with it. 'Intimacy is an important word for me. Through awareness we can learn to be intimate with nature, with the elements, and with our bodies – in the same way as we think of developing intimacy with another person. That intimacy opens us to the sense of presence and humanity here, right now, in this moment. That intimacy with life lies at the heart of what it is to be human.'

The same quality of awareness without detachment has prompted Christopher's peace work, the practical corollary of his arguments in *Transforming our Terror*. He has travelled for many years to Israel and the West Bank where he works closely with the peace movement and others on both sides of the divide. 'Recently I gave a public talk in Tel Aviv, and I said, "The Israeli military must get out of the West Bank, and allow the Palestinians to live their lives. Soldiers must refuse to support the occupation."

'One man came up to me afterwards, very angry, and asked, "Who do you think you are to come here and tell us what to do? What do you know about the situation?" I asked him, "How many Palestinians have you met and asked what their lives are like?" I could see from his face that he had never spoken to any; so I said, "I go and listen to the nightmare of the Palestinians, as well as hear from Israelis about their sorrow. That is my authority to speak on such matters."'

How can a Buddhist mediate between Jews, Muslims, and Christians in the Middle East? Christopher emphasizes that he isn't looking for converts. 'I tell people, "You already have three religions, the last thing you need is a fourth!" I guide people in looking at their responses and their minds, and sometimes they want to know more. So I have been asked to lead retreats in Israel, making available the Buddha's insights, but without any expectation that people will become Buddhists.

'It is a delicate position. In Nablus, where I give workshops on the resolution of suffering, the Palestinians know I am totally supportive of their right to liberation, independence, and to live in peace, and the Israelis know that I am wholly supportive of their right to exist.'

Listening to others parallels the act of listening to oneself in meditation, and Christopher advocates an open questioning attitude: 'How do we find a different way of looking? How do we witness what is happening without taking sides? What leads us to believe and accept a particular version of reality?' Such questioning points to the Buddhist emphasis on examining and letting go of divisive views. 'According to the Buddhist texts, the Buddha again and again asks us to look at our views,' Christopher commented. 'This isn't the same as being non-judgemental – which is what so many Western Buddhists are advocating. The Buddha was always criticizing the views that were prevalent in his society, saying they led people into suffering. Far too many Buddhists live in fear of appearing judgemental. There is an inability to distinguish between critical, passionate analysis and heaping blame upon others. The first step on the Noble Eight-fold Path is Right View, not timid view, not comforting view, and not non-view.'

Among the reflections Christopher is most keen to promote is the contemplation of birth, ageing, pain, and death to generate love and compassion amid the vulnerability of daily life. 'In vipassanā monasteries in Asia you can see corpses, sometimes those of senior monks or lay people, to remind you of the truth of impermanence. Contemplating death is the most profound meditation because it has the power to cut through all your ideas about yourself, your plans, your self-importance. Everything you get caught up with and think matters.'

Christopher is convinced that such meditative insights have much to offer the political domain. 'However sophisticated our technology, the level of emotional maturity guiding the political courses of our countries is low. There is no attempt to under-stand the "other", to ask how others see us and what we may have done to prompt their anger. Until we can look inside and see how we deal with our own anger and forces of destruction (often disguised by politicians and others as making hard deci-sions about the real world), we will continue to see its painful consequences in the world outside us.'

Above all, this entails honest, rigorous self-inquiry. As he writes, 'A major catastrophe gives us the opportunity to enquire into our relationship with our beliefs, feelings and opinions. It also acts as a metaphor for other situations of conflict or a seemingly insoluble position.'

For all the positivity of its message, *Transforming our Terror* is pervaded by sadness that, far from seizing this opportunity, our political leaders chose to hurl themselves into a cycle of punish-ment, retribution, and the attempt to control. What can one do in response? Christopher's activism has made him a veteran of Dharma *yatras*, or peace pilgrimages, which are walked in many countries.

Along with a teaching programme in which he led meditation retreats on four continents, Christopher's activism makes him an incessant traveller who draws breath when he lands back in his beloved Totnes. I leave him at the station, scarf trailing behind him. He is off to his daughter's house, then on to his reg-ular window seat in the local coffee shop. There he sits, as he has for several years, meeting and engaging with old friends, Dharma students, or anyone who wants to chat, with a warm greeting and a welcoming smile.

This image of Christopher encapsulates his message for meditators, politicians, and all of us who need to absorb our ex-perience, with its many difficulties – staying open, not closing down, and bearing witness to whatever life brings.

warrior of love

Joan Halifax Roshi
profiled by Vajrasara

Joan Halifax Roshi looks good for a warrior. With her shaved head, delicate bones, and charming smile, she appears younger than her 62 years. Yet she has been striving for the good for decades – long before she became a Zen abbot.

As a young activist in the 1960s, she was involved in the American civil rights and anti-war movements. She has been an anthropologist, academic, author, campaigner, prisoners' counsellor, and Dharma teacher. For thirty-five years she has supported individuals with life-threatening illnesses, and she is the founder of the Project in Being with Dying. She has worked with indigenous peoples in Asia and the Americas on environmental and health issues, and with native approaches to healing. In 1990 she founded Upaya Zen Center, where she teaches Buddhism and trains those caring for the dying.

Roshi Joan's interest in Buddhism began in the mid 1960s, at a time when young westerners were questioning many aspects of the human mind and society. 'I wasn't originally magnetized to Zen per se, it was just what I encountered. I read Alan Watts and D.T. Suzuki and felt intuitively that I was a Buddhist. I was at Columbia University at the same time as Thich Nhat Hanh. I admired his approach to nonviolence, so from 1965 I became a "book Buddhist" – I had no teacher and taught myself to meditate from a book.'

In 1975 she met her first teacher, a Korean Zen master called Seung Sahn. 'He was energetic, brilliant, and radical. I studied under him for ten years and learned so much.' She gradually felt she needed more of an engaged approach; so she spent ten years as a student of Thich Nhat Hanh, and became a member of the Order of Interbeing. 'After another decade I wanted an American teacher and Bernie Glassman's views were more congruent with my own. So for the past ten years Glassman Roshi has been my teacher.' Under Glassman Roshi she became a roshi and a founding teacher in the Zen Peacemaker Order. 'I've benefited from all three teachers tremendously.'

A vision of discipline and elegance, Roshi Joan wears a brown Zen kesa over a Chinese-style black robe, beneath which is a white Japanese kimono. There is a fastidiousness about her; she regularly adjusts the hang of her kesa, and the fold of her robes – perhaps because of the Zen emphasis on precision and ritual form.

'In one way my priest's robes are very symbolic, part of a lineage going back two and a half thousand years. And, being a woman, it's also a profound political statement – given that women have a growing role in the spread of Buddhism today. On the other hand, we must not get too caught up in the identity of being a teacher.' She picks up the fabric and shrugs. 'It's only eleven yards.'

It was her grandmother who first inspired Roshi Joan to work with dying people. 'Familiarity with sickness and death was part of my upbringing, as my grandmother cared for the dying in her neighbourhood in Georgia, so it seemed a natural path for me.' She began working with the dying in 1970 as a medical anthropologist in the Miami School of Medicine. Buddhism definitely influenced this work from the start. 'For example, the teachings on impermanence, selflessness, and the importance of contemplating one's own mortality. Also Buddhist meditation practices have increasingly given me more stability in terms of offering care and presence to dying people.'

As an anthropologist she studied indigenous religions, particularly shamanism. She focused on the psycho-spiritual crisis of death and rebirth through which the shaman passes, and the approach of shaman as healer. She has also written several books on the subject. 'This all fed into a life that has been influenced by my father's compassion and my mother's service. My mother was a volunteer her whole life. Right up to the day she died she was still delivering magazines and books to dying people in hospital.'

When Joan married the psychiatrist Stanislav Grof, she began to work in his project with people dying of cancer. 'That work gave me a tremendous impetus. I saw that dying people were the most marginalized in the American hospital system. And I wanted to respond.' Their research led to them writing a book: *The Human Encounter with Death*.

'After Stan and I divorced I just continued my work. I was researching all religions, looking for the "methodology", instructions that could support dying people, and help us all to prepare for death. As my Buddhist commitment deepened, I discovered that Buddhism has so much to offer in this regard.'

Since then, she has been offering care and presence to the dying, especially those with AIDS, and training others in contemplative care. She also worked in a New Mexico jail with maximum-security prisoners and men on Death Row. 'I've always been drawn to people in catastrophic situations. It makes me more vigilant, more patient. Something about the acuteness of their situation encourages transparency. However, I wouldn't have predicted this would become my life's work, nor that I'd be one of the pioneers in this field.'

Roshi Joan asserts that being with people who are close to death or in prison is life-saving. How so? 'On a superficial level it makes me grateful for my own life and health; it helps me to get my priorities straight. On a deeper level I get to practise presence in the face of old age, sickness, and death more immediately than in any context I can imagine.'

Her advice to everybody is to spend time with those who are dying, and to step inside a prison – and find out who you are in those situations. 'You see how you, too, are dying, and how you, too, are in your own prison. How you're perhaps only one thought away from being in a physical prison.'

After years of experience, is she better able to cope in the face of death and dying? 'When a close friend dies I'm more likely to allow myself to feel the loss deeply now; I can let go into the experience, knowing that it's impermanent. So in one sense I'm much more emotionally resilient. Those who see me with dying people think I'm very strong, and maybe it's true. But I'm also more sensitive around death, less numb, and in that way less resilient. I've seen so much suffering and haven't always been able to let go of it. So it cuts both ways. I'm pretty human in all of this.'

One example she gave was a long-standing friend whom she had promised to be with at his death. But when he developed cancer he was raging against the prospect of dying. 'Lying in hospital, he was furious and fired everyone. He told us all to fuck off. A small part of me was heartbroken, but mainly I didn't take it personally. I realized I couldn't help him, but I could help his family who were very traumatized by it. If one can stand steady and kindly, and not take the abuse personally, one may be a real help. I also managed to support the nurses – I bore witness to their disgruntlement – and made a few jokes to help them release. So I did the best I could.'

Roshi Joan is keen that dying people are allowed to be fully themselves, 'not overly arranged' by those around them. She also warns against the myth of a spiritual death: 'I find the notion of a "good death" problematic. We mustn't coerce someone into dying in the way we hope. Death is not dignified. It hardly ever turns out how we anticipate, or how we wish. Just before my father died he started flailing about, so we had him medicated, partly because he was injuring himself in his agitation, and partly for us, his family. I could barely stand it, and wanted to do anything to make him peaceful.'

Until 1994, Roshi Joan was running individual programmes with the dying across North America and abroad. Then she realized she needed to consolidate and share her expertise, so she established the Project in Being with Dying, teaching professional care-givers how to be with the dying process.

This training programme – for doctors, nurses, hospice workers, pastoral carers, and so on – is drawn from Roshi Joan's research, experience, and spiritual practice. 'The knowledge in Buddhism that has arisen from the determined and intelligent exploration on the part of meditation adepts over the centuries has yielded a treasury of practices. These are accessible to us and can really transform our experience of living and dying.'

When setting up this project, she asked the Dalai Lama which qualities he felt she would most need. He replied, 'A big heart, great determination, and,' he paused, 'probably hardest for you – a lot of patience.'

She roars with laughter, 'But I'd only just met him! Am I so easy to read?'

The Tibetan tradition is rich in practices that can assist the dying and those caring for dying people. For example, the Nine Contemplations of Atīśa, *tonglen*, *phowa*, dream yoga, reflection on the dissolution of the body, and of course the teachings of the *bardo*, are all used in training. 'Actually it'd be good for everyone to practise these – before they reach that critical stage!' Many of these meditations and reflections require a stable meditation practice and a certain amount of self-awareness. However, most carers have never meditated, so more esoteric practices are not introduced on the initial training.

A range of people undertake the training, coming from as far as the Middle East and Europe, as well as Canada and Mexico. The majority are not Buddhists, but they aren't alienated by the programme – and many take up meditation afterwards. 'I've taken teachings from the whole Buddhist tradition and rewritten them to be less sectarian, more approachable – though still challenging – for westerners.' These are published in small books for anyone interested in the dying process.

'The course is deep and demanding. It's extremely well received, and many people repeat it.' With the publication of the curriculum and enough people being trained, Roshi Joan hopes she can 'leave this earth feeling a little better'. She'd like to see more physicians and nurses from the UK and Europe come over and do the training. There's so much enthusiasm for contemplative care in Europe that she'd like to establish a training group there.

One of the issues addressed in the training is that all carers (professionals and families) believe they haven't done enough. So they are encouraged to recall compassionate phrases, such as, 'May I be forgiven for not meeting my loved one's needs.' Caregivers clearly need to take care of themselves – keeping socially and spiritually alive. They also need strong boundaries: learning how to respond so they're not wiped out, and not fixed on how things will turn out.

'When offering care, exploration of a person's world-view is essential. As well as being a kindly presence, we try to heal that person's perception that they're separate and isolated. Do patients have a sense of impermanence? Or do they feel shame or guilt at having developed cancer?'

When sitting with a dying person, Roshi Joan believes it's helpful for the carer's quality of presence to be complete. 'We want to give our best, to be fully there. Compassion may move us, it can draw out the best in us, but it doesn't always! We must be unattached to the outcome. Either way, it's always edifying.'

It also calls for humility. 'I can't just walk into a hospital with my spiritual stuff, and assume I'll be a help. We need to engender compassion and equanimity, and take these out to the world. But we can only do that by facing our own complexes. Are we sitting with someone who's dying, or with ourself? We don't turn away from our own issues, just as we don't turn away from a dying person. It's tough. But that's where the rubber meets the road!'

For all her broad-mindedness, Joan Halifax had a narrow upbringing. She was raised in the American South into a sheltered Protestant community, which excluded Jews and Catholics, and blacks were only permitted as staff. Hers was a virtuous, loving family and she was sent to an Episcopal girls' boarding school, so her experience of life was very limited.

Having been brought up virtuous, Joan learned to be 'unvirtuous' in the 1960s. 'I enjoyed that era of sex, drugs, and revolution – and had my share of wild times. Even contact with Zen didn't immediately change that, because in those early days the Zen teachers I met were more iconoclastic; ethics weren't emphasized. Only later did I realize the important foundation that an ethical life provides. Since then I've been relearning virtue!'

She propounds what she calls Compassionate Zen. A student once suggested that Compassionate Zen was an oxymoron, a contradiction in terms. She laughs. If so, Roshi Joan is a living, breathing oxymoron. Active compassion has always been central to her life, and in the zendo a statue of the bodhisattva of compassion, Kuan Yin, has a prominent place.

Her teaching is peppered with political comments and references to current events, as well as amusing anecdotes and tales of her travels. Sitting opposite her, I have a strong sense of the urgency she feels for us all to wake up – and respond to human suffering and environmental degradation. She encourages students to develop the ability to sit with their own and others' pain. Not to shrink from doing difficult things but to work on deepening their character. 'Give life to life,' she urges repeatedly.

Outspoken and passionate, Roshi Joan has created a few waves over the years. When discussing loss of reputation, she smiles, 'Been there, done that.'

Have there been any major incidents?

'Nothing particular. I've attracted my share of criticism – perhaps inevitably, being unconventional, a woman, and as vocal and determined as I am. I've received lots of advice and taken very little of it. I've been unmarried most of my life and, when I was younger, not as ethical as I might have been. I've made many mistakes – and suffered and learned from them all.'

True to her pioneering spirit, Joan Halifax is one of few women to have become a roshi. 'Ordination of women was unusual in the Zen tradition, but that's finally changing: a number of Western women are becoming acknowledged roshis, which I think is tremendous.'

'I took my celibacy vows having lived a full life, my priorities were clear and I wanted to serve the Dharma wholly. A sexual relationship takes care and time, so for me it didn't feel like renunciation – more a liberation. I'm having more joy and fun now than I ever did when breaking precepts at a much graver level. But I don't follow the Vinaya; it's too restrictive for the life I lead.'

She is, however, convinced of the value of a teacher. 'I've been meditating for forty years but you could discount the first ten years as I didn't have a teacher. I feel you really need a living teacher and clear spiritual guidance if you're serious about Dharma practice. I recommend finding a teacher who's been through the fires and made more mistakes than you – they'll have developed compassion as a result. Teachers are just human; they fall off the wagon sometimes. With Bernie Glassman, I've got a lot of bang for my buck. He's rough, demanding, and straight up.'

Although she has consistently followed the thread of Zen with three different teachers, Roshi Joan has explored many forms of the Dharma. She has been especially influenced by Tibetan Buddhism, with its emphasis on *bodhicitta*, and has benefited from contact with various Rimpoches in Asia and the West. She has also felt supported in her Zen practice by friendships with key American teachers in the Western vipassanā approach.

'In my practice I emphasize the teachings of the Buddha, which was unusual in Zen (though it's becoming more common in the West now). I value the systematic approach to meditation of the Theravādins. For example, I think the detailed meditation instructions in the *Ānāpānasati Sutta* are very helpful for Western practitioners. And I love the directness and rigour of Zen, so my Zen approach appreciates and draws on all major schools of Buddhism. I don't think it's too mongrelized, not so eclectic that it loses the point. The different traditions that I've explored have each strengthened my own Zen practice. It's given me greater perspective.'

Roshi Joan travels widely and juggles numerous campaigns and projects. For example, she is one of the founders of Mind and Life, the dialogue between the Dalai Lama and Western scientists. This group first met in 1983, and it was Mind and Life research which, among other things, recently revealed that Buddhist meditation makes people happier. 'It's an important initiative; it has also been a wonderful opportunity to be in His Holiness's presence.'

Yet for an activist she has a great capacity to turn inward, and has spent forty years developing her inner resources. The path of meditation suits her temperament. When she did a character analysis test she proved to be an introvert, to everyone's surprise but her own. 'I know how much I value solitude. I guess I'm an introvert with a personality!'

Her friends often advise her to do less, to lead a quieter life. 'But that's not my style. I'm here to help as many beings as I can in this life.' With her irrepressible energy and capacity to serve, she expresses altruism in numerous ways – not least as Abbot of Upaya Zen Center, New Mexico, founded in 1990.

Upaya is set amid the beautiful foothills and glorious clear air around Santa Fe. Roshi Joan meditates there three or four hours each day. 'I set up a monastery in order to make myself practise – and not avoid things through overwork. My students keep me at it. I'm in the zendo for every meditation session.' Upaya has fifteen full-time residents, and a number of Zen students come to practise for shorter periods. The resident students help to run the monastery. 'They're so kind and dedicated; we couldn't do anything unless we worked as a team.'

Her vision for Upaya was to establish a Zen training centre that emphasizes social service and social action. It was named Upaya because skilful means is a key concern. 'As Buddhists we practise with the attitude, "so you have pain, no big deal, it happens," because it's important that we develop equanimity in the face of suffering. But if you're with a bereaved relative after their loved one has died, you do not suggest it's no big deal. No way. Learning skilful means, being appropriate, is vital.'

According to one of her students, 'Roshi Joan is always bringing a radical edge to Buddhism that keeps Upaya vibrant and full of good works.' One of these good works is the Mettā Refuge programme, which makes it possible for people with catastrophic illnesses to come to Upaya for up to three weeks as a guest. 'It's a wonderfully supportive opportunity, and has been inspiring for our residents.'

At Upaya, the *Heart Sūtra* that is chanted is a translation by Roshi Joan. In this version the word *śūnyatā* is rendered 'boundlessness', rather than the usual 'emptiness'. This was because she found it hard to talk to dying people about emptiness – it had the wrong feel. Boundlessness implies both wide open and expansive, as well as non-dual and unfettered. 'Boundlessness suggests the process-oriented idea of discovering one's own boundless mind. I feel it's a much better word for westerners, especially those close to death.'

After meeting Roshi Joan, I was left with a lasting impression of her wholeheartedness. With a beaming smile, she's always urging people to give their all, give 100% energy to their Dharma training. 'As my Korean teacher used to say, 'It's like dynamite: 99% – no pow! With 100% – pow!' Roshi Joan certainly has pow!

_____*empathy for the devil*

Stephen Batchelor
interviewed by Dhivan

After *Buddhism Without Beliefs* became a US best-seller, Stephen Batchelor's publisher gave him free rein in his follow-up books. In 2000, having just moved to France with his wife to live as a freelance Buddhist writer and teacher, he started work on *Living with the Devil*. When I met Batchelor at the end of a visit to the UK, I wondered how he had come to this surprising subject.

'I had lots of material and notes that I'd always wanted to mould into a book, but it didn't have a theme. Within a few weeks, the material led me to Māra, the Buddhist version of the devil. I'd never been interested in him before, but I became fascinated and realized that I had the seed of a book. I started going into it in my usual obsessive kind of way, looking up every reference I could find, both within Buddhism and outside it in the Judaeo-Christian tradition, and that gave me my theme. I had no idea where it was going, and the writing emerged in the course of my struggle with the idea of Māra that I had had.'

I can relate to this. In the summer of 2003 I also found myself obsessed by the devil, having closely studied *Paradise Lost*, in which the poet John Milton famously gives Satan all the best lines. Where, I asked myself, is the devil in my own experience? It seemed to me that, despite my not holding a belief in God, I still related to morality, in terms of obedience to some kind of internalized authority figure. Satan, on the other hand, is the great rebel against thoughtless obedience. I wrote a series of poems in the voice of Satan, and ended up leading workshops on the theme of 'befriending Satan'. The point was not to start acting out one's shadow-side, but to acknowledge that the devil, the voice of instinctive self-centredness, is always there, always influencing us. We don't get far in the spiritual life by simply denying him; there has to be some conversation and integration.

In *Living with the Devil* Batchelor has quite a different approach, but he is addressing the same human situation. 'Some of the first material I wrote for the new book was a development of material that appeared years ago in a booklet called *Flight*, which was an afterthought to *Alone with Others*. I wanted to develop the idea that existential flight, which is the human tendency to flee from the difficult reality of experience towards distraction or entertainment, is a natural response to contingency. "Contingency" is how I translate *pratītya-samutpāda*, or dependent arising, the Buddha's fundamental teaching on the nature of reality.'

Batchelor's previous book, *Verses from the Centre*, was a poetic rendering of a work by the Buddhist philosopher Nagarjuna, in which this contingency is identified with *śūnyatā* or emptiness, the lack of essential identity in phenomena. *Saṃsāra*, the endless cycle of suffering, is, Batchelor might say, this flight from contingency. Instead of opening to the contingent, empty nature of things, we endlessly seek identity, security, and permanence. But this sets us in a vicious circle, since in our quest for happiness we are evading Reality. In German, Batchelor notes, a vicious circle is a *Teufelskreis*, a 'devil's circle': it is the devil who deceives us into circling, getting nowhere. In Buddhism this devil is called Māra.

'Māra', he tells me, 'is a way of talking about the contingent and imperfect structure of the world. A lot of Western Buddhists, and maybe Asian Buddhists too, tend to read Māra as a psychological function: as negative states of mind, attachments, grasping, and so on. This is only part of the picture. It fails to see that Māra is a metaphor for the very structure of the contingent world that is constantly breaking down and exposing you to death and the unpredictability of life itself. All that is Māra.'

The figure of Māra is familiar to most Buddhists as the trickster character who, in the traditional story, tries to prevent Siddhartha Gautama from attaining Enlightenment while he sits beneath the bodhi tree. Māra sends fearsome armies to assail the bodhisattva, and gorgeous daughters to tempt him back to worldly life. But Māra fails, the Buddha is victorious, and the defeated Māra slinks away, dejected.

I suggest that Māra represents something like the personality of *saṃsāra*. Batchelor agrees. 'I'm interested in how this figure can only work as a personality. As soon as you reduce it to something less than a personality, for instance to a psychological function, you lose sight of what it is essentially about. Māra means "killer", and Buddhist tradition speaks of the four *māras*. There's *kleśa māra*, the psychological compulsions that control you; *skandha māra*, the body-mind itself as fragile, as dying, as killing you; *yama māra*, death itself; and *devaputra māra*, the Māra that appears as the son of a god. But the tradition loses sight of Māra as a personality when he is reduced to these four functions. In the West he is reduced just to *kleśa māra*, the psychological function, to our destructive, negative, and limiting psychological states. Māra is the *kleśas*, of course, but he's not only that.

'The Buddha describes Māra as *antaka*, which means "the maker of limits". We have no trouble understanding this psychologically: if I'm in a state of anger or attachment, I'm limited, trapped. I'm in one of Māra's snares. It's harder to understand this in the context of our lives as a whole, but the fact is that our existence here is finite, so Māra is a metaphor of finitude. If I have a stroke, that will probably limit my capacity to realize those values I most deeply cherish. If I'm imprisoned by some tyrannical regime, that's Māra. Death is more obviously a limit to our freedom. So Māra is that which blocks my way in life, inhibits my capacity to realize my values and goals.'

In the traditional story of the Buddha's Enlightenment, once Māra has tried and failed to tempt the Buddha back to worldliness, his part is over: he is defeated. However, he crops up quite often in the early Pali *suttas*, appearing as a doubting voice, which the Buddha hears, acknowledges, then overcomes.

We talk about how orthodox this understanding of Māra is. In both Theravāda and Mahāyāna traditions, the figure of Māra quickly became the four *māras*, and was turned into a theological doctrine. Meanwhile, the figure of the Buddha was elevated to higher and higher degrees of perfection, as all-wise, all-loving, and so on, until he was effectively dehumanized, becoming completely devoid of limiting features apart from his human body.

'But the early tradition did preserve the sense that the Buddha exists in a constant tension with this counter-image, or shadow, called Māra, which I understand as his own conflicted humanity. That leads to my point – which is not at all orthodox – that Māra never goes away. Although the Buddha achieved a certain freedom, Māra was still around, whispering in his ear. But I don't have any sense that the Buddha was troubled by this. He was subject to temptation, you might say, subject to thoughts and feelings arising in his mind that we might call "self-doubt". This self-doubt appears as a personality – there is something very consistent about Māra's voice. It reminds me of Satan's voice in Milton's *Paradise Lost*. It's insidious; alternately extremely self-confident then un-self-confident, swinging from arrogance to despair.'

We talk about the character of Satan, the archetypal rebel, in Milton's poem. I suggest that the figure of Satan, who rebels against an omnipotent, omniscient, tyrannical God, is attractive because he represents something about our humanity, something imperfect yet magnificent in his courage and individuality. 'Māra is rebelling against Enlightenment,' adds Batchelor. 'Māra is that part of us which, when we sit in meditation, for example, does not want to watch the breath. I think Māra is our humanity. There's something touching about those passages in the *suttas* where Māra fails in his tempting of the Buddha.

'You lose sight of the Buddha when you delete Māra, because you lose sight of that part of the Buddha with which you can identify. You can see yourself in Māra much more easily than in the Buddha. And yet if you bring these two split-off parts back into a single image, the Buddha becomes humanized while Māra paradoxically becomes "Buddha-ized". In this sense, Māra is not just a problem, Māra is necessary for Enlightenment to happen. Māra is the problem without which there would be no solution.

'When I told others I was writing a book about the devil, most people came up with a story, an image, an anecdote that encapsulated their own particular sense of the devil. These were incredibly diverse, which suggests the complexity of the image. "Devil" is not a word in most Buddhists' spiritual vocabulary, and yet when you say it, it immediately evokes an intuitive response. It's an image that everyone connects to, in varied ways.

'To me, the Buddha and the devil, or Māra, are two modes of a single organism. The Buddha is the capacity of that organism to open, Māra is its capacity to shut down. And that is non-dualistic because there's only the one organism, the human being. Traditional Buddhism has succumbed to a dualism, that the Buddha is good, Māra is bad. The Buddha is perfectly good; in his idealized perfection, he is no longer quite human. Māra is this figure the Buddha overcomes. Good and evil are split off from one another in orthodox Buddhism.'

What then is Māra, in terms of this single organism? When does the devil appear in experience? I suggest that Māra reveals himself as one's Buddha-nature is revealed; the personality of the devil forms and begins to speak – as rebellion, as compulsion and obstruction – as one becomes aware of the possibility of awakening.

Batchelor continues, 'As soon as you make this foolhardy commitment to Enlightenment, you wave a red rag at the bull of Māra. When you decide, "I'm going to wake up", you're basically saying "no" to Māra, who, until that point, has been running the show. You are saying "no" to the deeply-seated, probably bio-neurologically rooted, tendency towards closure, attachment, desire, fear – the flight from staying open in a contingent world. As soon as you turn against that, you affirm your own possibility of becoming a Buddha but also expose the deep resistance you have to waking up. Māra is everything that resists awakening. So, yes, Māra only becomes apparent when you seek to break free of his control. Until that time you don't notice him; you just think, well, this is life.'

I'm interested in how this conception of Māra fits with modern theories of evolution. I suggest that the tendency of the human organism to close down and rest in its fixed sense of itself must have some usefully adaptive function, some advantage for survival.

'I think that's absolutely right, and makes perfect sense of *skandha māra*, the devil of psychophysical existence. Along with my unorthodox conception of Māra goes a relinquishing of beliefs in karma and rebirth. I find it far more convincing to think that greed, hatred, and delusion, the classic Buddhist baddies, are legacies of early and advantageous biological survival strategies than to consider them as impressions on the stream of mind carried over beginningless lifetimes. This biological account of the origin of greed, hatred, and delusion seems far more convincing than the traditional metaphysical one, and it explains why Māra keeps appearing to the Buddha. The Buddha is still in his evolutionarily-driven organism; he still has his reptilian brain and Māra is built in to the organism itself.'

This image of the devil as belonging inseparably to our biological nature leads us to a discussion about the nature of Enlightenment: does freedom mean being completely free of greed, hatred, and delusion, or does it mean knowing them so well that they no longer dominate? The early scriptures offer images for both possibilities: the Buddha often ends his discourses by describing the three poisons as 'cut off like a palm stump, never to rise again'. But he also compares the Enlightened person to a rock on which a crow, representing Māra, can no longer gain any purchase. The crow just flaps dejectedly away.

'So freedom is achieved not by killing the crow but by making oneself such that Māra no longer has any hold on you. The Buddha says he has become invisible to Māra, and that makes sense to me, whereas the image of a cut-off palm stump suggests an act of violence against the psyche and the reptilian brain.

'Māra is what inhibits the freedom to be in-between. Usually we want to own and control whatever space we're in, and this leads to the "Māra-ization" of religion. The philosophy closes down. My thinking is self-consciously anti-orthodox by trying to open up another way of seeing the condition we're in. I consider myself a Buddhist – although some of my critics might question this – but I don't define myself exclusively in Buddhist terms, intellectually or spiritually. I'm concerned to address the postmodern situation that is our reality.

'We have the capacity to be plural, to enter into the world-views of Freud or Blake without difficulty, while practising Buddhism. The negotiation between world-views enriches us, or if it is confusing, that confusion can be good. This, too, is living with the devil. Up to the last moment, the book was going to be subtitled "a Buddhist meditation on good and evil", but just before it went to press I phoned my editor and said, "We have to get the B-word out."

'I think my approach puts me closer to the original Buddhist idea that life is *duḥkha*, suffering. The contingent world is a place that breaks us down and kills us. Buddhists often don't want to look at this; there's this great fear about demonizing nature; everything has to be brought back to "my mind" and its compulsions. We find it hard to make the link to Māra being death. Quite a lot of well-informed Buddhist friends have told me, "Māra's not death; Māra is our *fear* of death." They psychologize Māra, they internalize him in terms of their relationship to death, but I think you miss something crucially important when you do that.'

I suggest that Batchelor has re-demonized nature. 'That's right, in a way. Nature is what will destroy us, but nature is also what allows us the possibility of waking up. We have Buddha-nature and Māra-nature, at any moment we have the capacity to open up or close down. It's the same with this world in which we're embedded: it's both good and bad, it's not reducible to either good or bad. The habit of making the split, cutting off from nature, is part of our suffering.'

exploring bodhicitta

Manjusura

Late in September 2001 my friend Thomas drove me to a cottage on England's north Norfolk coast. I was beginning a two-week solitary retreat that I'd been longing for for several months. Tom helped me in and shared a pot of tea, and then he drove off, leaving me to an unfamiliar house, to the beach and woods nearby, and to two unplanned weeks. I had no idea what would emerge.

Since September 11th, radio, television and the Internet had reported the impending US retaliation for the attacks on the World Trade Centre and the Pentagon. There are several US army and air force bases in Norfolk, and there had already been some movement of troops and equipment. When I walked on the beach, I heard military aircraft flying high above the obscuring clouds. One day they circled out over the sea, back to land, and back out to sea for hours, their engines an ominous, ghostly roar, distant but deep and resonant, that seemed to fill the entire afternoon. On another evening, as the sun was setting, two fighter jets emerged from a break in the clouds, flying low and slow over the water, returning to base.

I had brought on retreat a book by Pema Chödrön, a Western Buddhist nun in the lineage of the Tibetan teacher Chögyam Trungpa Rimpoche. I had chosen this book because the title fitted how I was feeling: _When Things Fall Apart: Heart Advice for Difficult Times_. For the previous few months I had been occupied with the many tasks of running an urban Buddhist centre, and tired by trying to sort out difficulties in the men's community where I lived. Reading that book and being alone, I realized I'd been feeling sorry for myself. Later, when I told my friends what I realized on retreat, I held my hand up close to my face, so my palm grazed the tip of my nose. I realized with some shame that my own difficulties were in such close focus that I was incapable of seeing beyond them to take in the lives of people around me. Not that I was unconcerned, but my own suffering was in the foreground, and that made it harder to take in others, except in the most blurry, peripheral way.

I had also brought with me a Buddhist magazine with a headline article on the subject of *bodhicitta*. It had attracted me from among the many magazines arrayed in a local bookshop – because across its cover was printed, 'Even ordinary people like us have this mind of Enlightenment called *bodhicitta*.'

Citta means 'heart' or 'mind'; *bodhi* means 'awake' or 'Enlightened' or, according to Pema Chödrön, 'completely open'. *Bodhicitta* is sometimes translated 'thought of Enlightenment', or – as in that headline – 'mind of Enlightenment', or 'heart of Enlighten-ment'; sometimes as 'awakening mind'. Sangharakshita, founder of the Order of which I am a member, translates it as 'the will to Enlightenment', by which he means that it is not just an idea or a thought, but 'an immensely powerful drive'. Over the years I have read about and heard several talks on *bodhicitta*, but it has always seemed remote – concerning rescuing beings from suffering. That seemed a grand and distant aspiration to which it felt naive and presumptuous for me to aspire. I had heard people discussing the best context for the 'arising of the *bodhicitta*', as though that would be a huge surge of energy shooting up through my body, or through the floor of a ware-house or shop where Buddhists were working together, and the world would never be the same again. Something in me switched off when people started speaking about the *bodhicitta*. It seemed 'not yet relevant' to me.

That was partly why I was drawn to that headline, 'Even ordinary people like us have this mind of Enlightenment called *bodhicitta*.' I had decided that ordinary people like me couldn't understand the *bodhicitta* and should just get on with trying to lead a harmless life. So, while I'd heard such pronouncements, I hadn't paid them much heed.

But somehow the events I'd witnessed on television on September 11th, and subsequently pored over in newspapers and magazines, had shifted something inside. And as the first week of my retreat passed, I became aware of how I had been affected by what I had seen and heard. Those events that had wrenched apart other lives had touched my own. This was mainly as a reminder of the vulnerability of my own life and the lives of people I love. These events felt much more immediate than most disasters, having happened in a culture that resembles my own. But chaos and human suffering are pervasive: the life – at least the stability, happiness, and health – of everyone, everywhere, is always under threat. The images of people much like myself leaping from the 100th floor of a building reminded me of the terrible fragility of the human body, and I could easily imagine myself in a similar position. With reflection, my awareness of this vulnerability seemed to spread wider and wider. I reflected that every day thousands of people die in pain and fear, whether in accidents, at the hands of other humans, through cataclysms of nature, or through disease.

Although I didn't really know what it was, I sensed that *bodhicitta* was what I needed – that in this concept that had so long confused me I would find guidance. The magazine article described *bodhicitta* as 'a place as vulnerable and tender as an open wound'. This was so different from my own understanding. Having seen *bodhicitta* as a remote aspiration, I hadn't taken in its aspect of tenderness. I was focusing on the distant goal, not what it would feel like to want to aspire towards that goal. This image of an open wound made sense to me, though, because the world suddenly felt more vulnerable. I hadn't understood that *bodhicitta* is about not just aspiration, but also action – how we respond to suffering in the world.

I decided I would work to understand *bodhicitta*, and since my way of being in the world is oriented towards writing, I realized that this would be through writing about it. I thought of the opening of the *Bodhicaryāvatāra*, a text by an eighth-century Indian monk called Śāntideva, which I have studied and always sensed to be an important book for me, though I never understood why. Śāntideva writes that his text will not say anything new, but that he is presenting these teachings 'to perfume my own mind'. I decided while on retreat, at a time when my heart was tender, that I would write about *bodhicitta* as a way of understanding it myself, and of 'perfuming my mind'.

Returning to the idea of my vision being blocked by my difficulties, I recalled that Śāntideva also used the image of a hand. He described how we automatically reach down to protect an injured limb, and asked why we don't usually respond with the same immediacy and concern when it isn't our own but another person's limb that is hurt. He then wondered, 'Why can I not also accept another's body as my self?' And he resolves that, 'in the same way one desires to protect oneself from affliction, grief, and the like, so an attitude of protectiveness and compassion should be practised towards the world.'

In Tibetan tradition, *bodhicitta* is described as having two aspects: relative and absolute. Absolute *bodhicitta* is seen as an aspect of, and sometimes as equivalent to, Enlightenment itself. Relative *bodhicitta* is spoken of as a disposition and an orientation for practice – the 'attitude of protectiveness and of compassion' that Śāntideva describes. I think it is with this distinction between absolute and relative *bodhicitta* that my confusion arose. Relative *bodhicitta* eluded me, and along with it the practice orientation that makes it meaningful day by day. I had thought of *bodhicitta* as a goal, one of those distant no-goals of the Mahāyāna, so I was unable to engage with the practice of *bodhicitta*, the work of cultivating an 'attitude of protectiveness and compassion', of realizing my connection to other beings and seeing beyond myself.

Early on in my Buddhist practice, I understood that practising the Buddha's teaching involved cultivating wisdom and compassion. I remember reading that these qualities were the two sides of the coin of Enlightenment. But I discovered that it is possible to engage with compassion as a useless ideal, a theoretical caring that remained in the realm of thought, seldom translating into real concern for the lives of people around me. The scholar Paul Williams makes an interesting distinction in his book, *Mahāyāna Buddhism*: 'A purely spiritual compassion is of very limited use and benefit.' By 'purely spiritual' I understand 'as opposed to practical'. And then Williams asks, 'Why should the compassion of a great bodhisattva be limited only to the spiritual?' An abstract compassion that makes no difference on a daily level is hardly useful or beneficial. Dilgo Khyentse Rimpoche made a similar point. 'Compassion by itself is not enough; [beings] need actual help.'

Buddhism asserts that mind precedes all things. So mind is the fundamental level on which we must approach the cultivation of compassion. This is a slightly knotty point: surely if actual help is needed, then we must do something useful to relieve others' suffering? But people rush off to war zones for all kinds of wrong reasons – sometimes with motivations that have more to do with their own psychology than any compassionate impulse. War zones aside, people try to help in everyday situations for reasons other than those they reveal, or even acknowledge to themselves. Training the mind towards compassion includes clarifying our motivations, becoming aware of what needs doing, then cultivating a genuine longing to help.

I have found one practice outlined by Śāntideva in the *Bodhicaryāvatāra* particularly effective. 'Whoever longs to rescue quickly both himself and others should practise ... exchange of self and other.' There are several formulations of the 'exchange of self and other' as a formal meditation practice, but all share imaginatively identifying with and taking on the hardships of other beings, and sending to them all our positive qualities, and our freedom, security, and pleasures. The way I have approached this practice derives from the Tibetan *lo-jong* or mind-training tradition, and is known as *tonglen* or 'sending-and-taking'. The meditation involves breathing in the sufferings of beings, which one visualizes as black smoke, then breathing out to them a bright, pure light. It's a simple practice, but it dramatizes the desire to identify with others.

I was reintroduced to this practice a few months before my retreat, having first encountered it ten years ago when I began practising with a Tibetan Buddhist group. At that time, I had found it simply too confronting – I felt unable to hold the degree of suffering that I saw and imagined in the world. In Norfolk I started slowly, by introducing ten or fifteen minutes into other meditation practices I was doing daily. This was enough for me to notice a feeling of my heart opening wider.

Pema Chödrön elaborates the tradition in recommending what she refers to as 'on-the-spot *tonglen*': a moment-by-moment identification with others. She says that the formal meditation practice is simply a reminder to practise spontaneous *tonglen*. When we notice a desire to pull away from another person, or to protect ourselves from a situation we find frightening or uncomfortable, or when we feel a painful emotion, we shouldn't immediately follow the impulse to escape. Rather, we should try to stand our ground, and then practise well-wishing, which we can visualize as taking in dark smoke and giving out pure light.

For me, this has been an effective, though often difficult, way to lower the hand that obscures my vision. That is not to claim that I've managed to put that hand to useful work in the world of suffering beings, but occasionally I have seen beyond it, just enough to respond appropriately to another person. Or at least I haven't strengthened my tendency to self-protection and isola-tion by pulling away from them. Travelling on the London Underground a few weeks ago, a tattered, strong-smelling man settled down beside me. My first thought was to find another seat; it took an act of will to remind myself that he wanted the same things from life that I want, to remain open, and not to run away. So I practised on-the-spot *tonglen*, and I saw that it does have an effect.

An appropriate response doesn't necessarily involve doing something. It can simply mean staying with a difficult or uncom-fortable situation. This seems to go against the points made by Williams and Dilgo Khyentse, but I am discovering the impor-tance of seeing suffering without pulling away. Before we can help, we have to learn just to look.

At about five-to-ten one morning I switched on the kettle. Tom is a man of his word, and the doorbell rang as the clock struck ten. As we had initiated my retreat with a shared pot of tea, so we now closed it, Tom filling me in on events in Cambridge. As we drove back I tried to communicate the themes that had emerged from the retreat, beginning by holding my hand close up to my face.

More recently, on a trip to Manhattan, I spent time walking slowly through the area around the World Trade Centre. There is to those streets a sense of irretrievable loss. In his book *Shambhala: The Sacred Path of the Warrior*, Chögyam Trungpa discusses *bodhicitta* in a chapter entitled 'The Genuine Heart of Sadness'. 'The genuine heart of sadness comes from feeling that your ... heart is full. You would like to spill your heart's blood, give your heart to others'; and, 'this experience of sadness ... occurs because your heart is completely exposed.' Identifying with another person, really suffering with them (the root mean-ing of 'com-passion'), Trungpa suggests, is the basis for *bodhicitta*.

In New York I found it easier than usual to do the meditation practice I was given at ordination, which involves visualizing the thousand-armed form of the bodhisattva Avalokiteśvara. Meditating one afternoon while riding the ferry across Hudson Bay back to Staten Island, I could easily visualize the bodhisattva in the clear sky over Manhattan, his thousand arms radiating around his body, reaching out to beings in need. Each arm ends in a hand opened in the gesture of giving, and in the centre of each hand is a wide-open eye, which is said to see the particular suffering of each being, enabling the bodhisattva to respond appropriately.

This strikes me as a fitting image for what my work entails. It involves bringing down the hand that habitually obscures my vision, and slowly transforming it into the wide-open, clear-seeing hand of the bodhisattva.

_____killing rage the zen punk way

Brad Warner

Akron, Ohio, February 1982. It's way below freezing outside, but in here it's so hot I feel like I'm going to melt into a puddle on the floor. I stand, legs akimbo, sticker-encrusted Musicmaster bass in hand, on the slightly raised platform near the bar at the Dale, a tiny pub near Akron University. Every dilapidated muscle in my undernourished body is flexed and ready for action.

'Drop the A-bomb on meeeee!' Jimi Imij, shaven-headed lead singer of Zero Defex shrieks as drummer Mickey X-Nelson counts in the beat and Tommy Strange and I attack our guitars. A mass of furious fuzztone erupts from the amplifiers and the pit comes alive with surging bodies smashing into each other like a forty-car collision. Eighteen seconds later the song is over. An uneasy calm, like a cease-fire just about to be called off, falls over the crowd for a few tense seconds until Jimi shouts 'Die Before More of This!', the title of the next song. We launch into another feedback-laden aural assault and the crowd is free once more to pummel each other bloody.

The American hardcore punk movement of the early 1980s was all about anger. We were pissed off at the senile B-movie actor who'd somehow been elected President. We were mad as hell at the Bible-thumping lunkheads who wanted to curtail all forms of free speech. We were enraged at the mind-numbing complacency of a generation of vacant-eyed mall rats – our so-called peers – who didn't seem to notice that we were being led down the path towards global Armageddon.

At the same time, I was screaming my lungs out at hypocrisy, greed, and bad fashion; I was also discovering Zen Buddhism, a philosophy that said the best thing you could do for world peace was to sit with your legs twisted up like a pretzel and stare at a wall. You could hardly find two more seemingly contradictory philosophies. Even so, I never felt the desire to leave behind my punk rock ways in order to follow the path of Zen. If anything, I'm more punk now than I was back then. At their core, both punk and Zen share some important key criteria. They are both about action in the present moment, about doing something right now, and about taking responsibility for your own life. The reason the punks believed they had to vent their anger was that they hadn't followed their own philosophy of totally rejecting society right to the end. They were still reacting to anger the way society told them to. And yet, sometimes shouting 'Drop the A-bomb on meeeee!' is the most Buddhist thing you can do. There's a vast difference between art about anger and anger itself.

So what does one do about anger? When I first heard one of my Buddhist teachers say that anger should be suppressed, it sounded not only absurd but positively unhealthy. Everyone knows you don't bottle up your anger, you let it out. Now I can see what he meant. When I looked a little more carefully it became apparent that anger wasn't some substance that built up inside of me and which I could 'let out' and be rid of. There was nothing in which anger could be bottled up. The process of letting anger out was actually the process by which more anger was produced.

Since meditation is all about understanding the state you're in here and now – and since I was often consumed with black rage as I sat on my black cushion – I've often focused my attention during zazen practice on understanding the real source of anger. It took a long time to see anger for what it was, and when I did I was truly shocked.

You'll sometimes hear the idea that our emotions are the things that keep us human. They are not. Our emotions – all of them – get in the way of our experiencing what it really is to be human.

I'd always believed that anger was somehow something apart from myself, that 'I' experienced 'my' anger. But as my Zen practice deepened it began to dawn on me that this was not the case at all. It wasn't that I could eradicate those qualities about myself I'd labelled as negative, while leaving the good stuff intact, like cutting off the rotten parts of a carrot left in the fridge too long and cooking the rest. I had to die completely. The source of anger, hatred, and fear was the same as the source of that collection of ideas and habits I had mistakenly called 'me' for most of my life.

It isn't just anger and other so-called 'negative' states that are the problem. It is that whole collection of things you call your 'self'. The very same force that makes it possible for you to gush all over a fuzzy little puppy dog with icky sweet love is the force that makes it possible for you to hate with passion and lash out with anger. There is no love without hate, no happiness without depression. It's like a roller coaster. If you go up, you're gonna have to come back down.

Hate can be your teacher. Anger can be your guide. It's a mistake to try and overcome them with emotions that seem to be their opposites. Emotions all stem from the same source. See your anger for what it is and then you can see yourself for what you are. And yet there is something else.... For want of a better term, I'll call it joy.

Joy is not bliss, by the way. Bliss is what you get from a heroin overdose. Numbness is numbness no matter how many 'spiritual masters' tell you it's bliss. Joy cannot be willed into being by thought or by cultivating vague memories of past experiences of it, even if those experiences were real. It comes only when body and mind are in perfect balance, and – more importantly – when we are at perfect balance with our own circumstances, when we no longer fight against reality. Not fighting against reality doesn't mean mindlessly accepting the way things are without trying to change anything. In fact, the only way to change your circumstances is to stop fighting them. To do this we have to understand clearly what we really are at every moment.

If you're serious about transcending anger you must be willing to give up everything. I'm afraid most people – including many who say they're Buddhists – are not at all serious about it. We've invented a million clever methods of building up our ego while pretending to tear it down.

If you learn to appreciate and fully experience each and every moment just as it is, anger will become less and less of a problem until it finally disappears entirely. Anger begins very small. It's always based upon the difference between how you think things should be and how they actually are. Within this gap, the fiction known as 'you' appears and reacts. In order to protect this fiction, you start to justify your anger, to build a convincing case to prove to yourself you have the right be angry. This can happen quickly, so it's important to stay right on top of it. To repress anger consciously means you do not allow yourself any excuses. You do not accept any of the justifications for anger your ego coughs up, no matter how reasonable you can make them sound. This is the only way to reach the source of anger and be finished with it completely.

I fought hard against this, like an alcoholic fights against the realization that the only way to stop being an alcoholic is just to stop drinking. He can no longer fool himself with the idea that he can drink today and then quit tomorrow. I could no longer pretend it was OK to get angry today about some situation in which I was clearly in the right as long as I didn't get angry at my girlfriend when we argued.

Anger always stems from the belief that you are right and your circumstances are somehow 'wrong'. When you think you're right – when you know for certain you're right – in the face of circumstances that are somehow 'wrong', that's when you need to look hard at what's actually happening inside. Your habit of reacting with anger has been built up over long years of reinforcement from a society gone terribly wrong. Society is made up of people, all clinging to the fiction of ego, who draw support for this idea from the fact that so many others believe it.

But you have to take this all the way … as far as it can go. You can't stop at anger. You have to see love, kindness, selflessness, and compassion the same way. Your ideas of these 'positive' states can be just as much of a hindrance as anger.

It's a dire mistake to view our ordinary state as a thing we can somehow fix by forcing it to conform to a self-invented ideal. If we don't clearly understand our own delusions – including the delusions we call 'positive', we'll never know if what we label as 'love' is the real deal or just another fantasy thrown up by our over-stimulated imaginations. Anger arises out of the belief in the individual self. When there is no 'you' there is nothing for 'you' to get angry about, and nobody outside yourself to feel angry with.

_facing the present

Danavira

I grew up in the West, a viewer risen to maturity in the great TV land. Perhaps you would have recognized yourself in me as I sat, an armchair plunderer of culture, before the screen, comfortable in the electron light, watching phenomena boxed-up, devised to entertain or enlighten me. You too may remember the glazed eye, the overcome mind, the in-drawn process of stultification that sprang from a world being passed before us, untouchable, and as such barely felt.

I could not count the faces I have seen searching the camera, in anguish, for pity, and finding none. Out of their lives they stared, from shadows and light, on cinema or television screen, into the density of my heart. Looking back, I think of it as a leech ing away of my human sensibility and feeling, a numbing down into a cloud of dreams through insubstantiality, mere visuals without embodiment, that fed a slow process of death by images. Thus I too was plundered of myself.

There was a time when, out of the wintering of my mind, I thought that war was fun and the blood spilled somehow a masquerade. 'Nam' was on the news each night when I was young. It happened far away. I loved the turning, distant jet, the dropping bomb, the jungle drawn up through flame, bringing exhilaration. Spectral field reporters told me with a glittering pity how bad it was and yet, perhaps, how necessary. My family was not in flames. We would sit there watching at our evening meal, enduring the explosions, followed by sport.

179

The puppet-like dead, made into blinded masks, I passed over safely contained within my eye of inevitability. They lay for the camera, a glance backwards set on their faces, from a gaze so turned away, dead flesh upon the bed of its catastrophe, forming a fierce norm in the life of their times. Already these were post-war streets, stained with memories of previous horror, peopled with the detritus of tragedy and the hard act, which cursed the familiar. So many naked lines, so many heaps, so many piles of separation were expressed as the world.

My boy's heart trembled. I cried but could not fill this brutal silence. The past was not mere memory, I saw. Each evening news laid out the present on the previous dead. All were related in my mind, none without consequence. It was as if the sunlight fell on ruins. There was a nihilistic splendour. MAD was the acronym of our security. Such were the cities of the West from which I've sprung. It is my time and still I will uphold it.

I grew up in the twentieth century and I praise it. It is the time of my life and I rejoice in it. I know as well as anyone the harm we human beings have done to ourselves and this planet, and ourselves, but it is now that I live and here that I exist, and I will not condemn it. Nor do I praise it unduly. This place, this time, is full of imperfections yet with potential to grow and develop. It is perfectible. I do not see it as a time of degeneration and hence destruction but as one in which change itself is a major social and cultural paradigm. This change cuts all ways and can be experienced by some as discomfort, and by others as happiness. The world I inhabit and I, myself, then, are imperfect yet perfectible. Apart from water no ice, outside living beings no Buddhas. To a Buddhist, all our troubles are seen as mud – it is from mud that the lotus grows.

I see in my mind how all the lives of this past time crowd in, to show themselves more clearly where they have always been, each a quantum of the moment. This moment of my life is lived in the grasp of their consequences. My face and yours bear the marks of their countless ills, their numberless oppressions. Their joy, too, is ours; in the light of our eyes is the light of theirs. Like them we have a reaching breath; it spills and seeds the world about us, making the process of an unknown future.

I am enfolded by such strangers, as I will become for those unborn. Everything I will have done shall fall as a basis for them, and I will be unknown, gone, too, a man of the silence. It is a great gift, to be and not to be, to be given all that I have, and to give. Thinking of our ancestors draws my heart beyond time, towards a fine knowledge. As if in the vastness of us all we stand, more than mere numbers in a count of mortality and fear but with a grand vision, capable of wonders.

It is hard to maintain this view. If even the gods tremble in the mundane world, seeing only so far and fearing farther, how much more so do our human minds, making up cycles of delight. I sigh in myself then for all our tragedies to come, for all the nestling wombs we will meet in places of misfortune, our future hellish states, our hearts both bestial and haunted, and our bewilderment on being born, merely to sicken, age and die upon the Wheel.

Yet my frail mind, drunk upon delusion, mistakes what is habitual, a shallow view, vague apprehensions, for a deeper truth. As such, I yearn after the flesh of the conventional. Those lines of common sense piled up in known heaps, the obvious truths, clear to the mature, in which we live and always have done, one heart poised against the other. Life means we dispose ourselves to live, in the simple-minded sense of a complex thing. Death stills our blithe way and proves our cheerfulness impaled, and we ourselves unstable – brittle, as Buddhist scriptures say, like an unbaked pot. Here we cling, making a heart in craving against the world, taking our appetites for wisdom.

Held in the sway of such insights, I hunger, reckless, after my desires and feel millennial marks upon my senses. In the press of our ancestors, in the weight of their consequences, who hungers through me? I reach out, intense, driven, backed by their times of bitterness or satiation, my selfishness wielding me like a knife, stabbing for a private future. From a palm-print on a cave wall until now, their hands and mine, five-fingered, the same – our grasp similar in intention as we state and restate patterns of culture. So can my mind be made a marionette to the generations if I am unaware?

To save myself I practise the Dharma. Through it I try to become more aware. I try to understand who or what I am. As such I go against this world in sensory flood, even as I love it. All those powerful effects that would make a mouth of me for their expression, I go against them. I need to intensify the focus of my mind for this, so that I witness what is pouring in and guard against mistakes. It was the vision of the Buddha that there is more to life than this state of wondrous drowning, within which we ordinarily live.

When I meditate, when I make myself more aware, I challenge history and the flow of past events. I loosen their grip. They cannot just wash over me and wash me away – a floating head in time, bobbing towards destruction. In going against that flow we collide. Out of the collision come new thoughts, feelings, knowledge, and sometimes insight. Through this process I become less numb and gain the chance to change my views.

In particular I practise the visualization of the bodhisattva Avalokiteśvara. What we visualize draws our mind and, where our mind goes, so does our life. When I visualize Avalokiteśvara I want consciously to move towards all that the bodhisattva represents. I want to embody these qualities. I want to bring them into the world where I exist, in this time. All these qualities could be encapsulated in one word: compassion. Avalokiteśvara is the bodhisattva of infinite compassion. So when I visualize I try to align my mind with the emanation of infinite compassion. By doing this I hope not only for a deeper understanding of life but to play my part in bringing blessings to the past, present, and future.

I choose for my ancestry everything that has ever been. All impersonal elements, in their clinging or eruption, I count as having made me. Creatures of every kind, dinosaurs and others, all who have lived and died and in their dying left descendants, they have made me. I praise this ageless impulse to be. It has given me this momentary brightness, a life with depths. Every race, all cultures, combine to make time an instrument of their gaze, in which I stand. Consciousness thus rains down from them, and everywhere the earth rises up in forms, works, services – the known.

Yet it is not enough. It has never been enough. The Truth aches in the structures of our minds. We seek release – and to know the Truth. We have a hunger then without weariness, endless, as if the unknown knowledges of our flesh had found a face in the stars, a net with which to fetch us in, beyond the labyrinths of daily life, its blind practices and repetitions, the beatings of a shallow heart. Drawn and driven, men and women everywhere have made their visions, thoughts, and ways of life in response. One such is the Dharma of the Buddhas. Embedded in this Dharma is Avalokiteśvara.

Avalokiteśvara has been worshipped and meditated on in many places, sometimes in male, sometimes female, form. His views transcend the ties of flesh and blood. He does not wear the blinkers I do. Through the history of the Dharma in this world many men and women have tried to align their minds with infinite compassion. It is a tradition beyond the normal bounds. I was not born to it. I took it up. When I practise, I align myself not only with the bodhisattva but with all those others who have practised, who are practising now. I feel supported by this and encouraged to continue. I want to be part of something greater than myself. It is obvious that connection with the bodhisattva leads this way. I want to put my energy behind a momentum for what is good, constructive. The vast momentum of Avalokiteśvara can be seen in statues or paintings of the bodhisattva.

Sometimes Avalokiteśvara has two arms, or four, eight, sixteen, or more – representing his ability to express the Dharma. The eleven-headed, thousand-armed Avalokiteśvara embodies this vast momentum most graphically. One thousand arms spread in immeasurable creativity, ready to help any living being. Eleven heads gazing out in a pillar of attention, scanning all directions of the world out of compassion.

The bodhisattva of infinite compassion has meditated deeply, seen the world in its nakedness and rich potential, and, with a heart set free, understands reality. I dress up daily in my senses. Taking my cue from ignorance, I mistake myself for form and in my foolishness I call myself substantial. The bodhisattva understands more deeply, and always as a friend. He sees beyond oppositions and desires, with such beautiful eyes, pure and clear. They are the friendliest eyes you will ever know: great pools of kindness and concern, emanating from vast depths.

Nothing disturbs such equanimity, such wise splendour. All that I fear, all that I cling to, is understood by the bodhisattva whose view is undefiled, steady, impervious to falsehood. My highest aspiration is heightened still by contact with his virtues. His perfect speech, whose skilful words allay all pain, speaks of nirvāṇa and the Great Awakening. Think of him without hesitation. Think of Avalokiteśvara, that pure being. In death, disaster, and calamity, he is the saviour, refuge, and recourse.

reflections
challenging times

notes on contributors

Aryadaka

Aryadaka was born in Seattle in 1948. Aged 20 he left the US to avoid being drafted into the Vietnam War, and while travelling through Europe and Asia he became a Buddhist. His meditation practice deepened when he was imprisoned in Finland in 1974 for 22 months. Shortly afterwards he met Sangharakshita, the founder of the Western Buddhist Order, and helped to create the London Buddhist Centre. In 1979 he returned to the US to care for his ailing father, and there he started Buddhist activities and married Sandra, his wife for the rest of his life. He was ordained within the WBO in 1984, established a flourishing Seattle Buddhist Center, and became America's first Buddhist prison chaplain. In 1997 he was diagnosed with hepatitis C and fell seriously ill. Unfortunately, the liver transplant described in his article did not save his life and he died in 2003, two years after the surgery.

Anna Cox

I am a clinical social worker in Little Rock, Arkansas and I have practised as a psychotherapist for over thirty years. Since the late seventies I have been a Buddhist practitioner, and this led me to doing volunteer work in prisons in Arkansas and around the US. I am the founder and president of Compassion Works for All, a non-profit organization that serves the most forgotten, especially those in prison, offering to prisoners a free spiritually and psychologically supportive and healing newsletter called *Dharma Friends*.

Danavira

I was born in Glasgow in 1949 to a Protestant father and a Catholic mother: I became a Buddhist. I joined the WBO in 1977, and if I have a main meditation practice it is working with the image of Avalokiteśvara. I live with my partner and have two children. I lead some events at the Buddhist centre in Cambridge, where I live, and I am a part-time student at a local college studying the history of the twentieth century, and cinema. I am trying to understand the times I have lived through and which shaped my mind. I think 56 is a good age to make such an intellectual effort. It also ties in with my life in the Buddhist community, which is not only a collection of people, but also a learning environment. Life is not something that it is possible to retire from.

Dhivan
The official story goes like this. I was brought up as a Roman Catholic in Somerset, England. An interest in meditation and yoga led me to the FWBO in Brighton in 1984, and a Goenka-style vipassanā retreat in India in 1986. I completed a Religious Studies degree at Lancaster University, specializing in Indian religions, and then a PhD in modern European philosophy. I have lived in Cambridge since 1997, working in team-based right livelihood (at Windhorse Trading and the Cambridge Buddhist Centre) and writing poetry and fiction. I presently live in a small residential community with other Buddhist men, and teach creative writing for Lancaster University, and Early Buddhism at the Cambridge Buddhist Centre. The unofficial story is that I am a fallen angel adapting to conditions on this strange and beautiful planet, with the Love Queen for companion and a heart full of sad songs. I prefer that one.

Robert Hirschfield
I grew up in a Jewish neighbourhood in the Bronx, New York, under a long shadow. Or, more precisely, under two long shadows. The shadow of the Holocaust, luridly engraved in my young mind, contributed to moulding me into a human rights journalist, whose subjects would include the holocausts in Cambodia and Sierra Leone. The shadow of my Aunt Anne's madness, punctuated by fiendish voices that she alone could hear, would take me in another direction: social work with mentally ill New Yorkers at a residence on the Lower East Side, and the unpaid job of care-giver for my Alzheimer's-stricken mother, a job I had for seven years; a job I continue to have, as I sit down each day to write my memoir of our lives together during those years. I came upon the Four Noble Truths, in my late thirties, as a result of those two shadows. Both are with me still.

Manjusura
I was born in Johannesburg in 1969. I taught Art History at the University of South Africa for a few years, then worked as a teacher-trainer. I published my first volume of poems in 1994, and a few years later co-edited an anthology of South African poetry for Penguin Books. I started meditating and exploring Buddhism when I was 16 or 17 years old, after reading *Zen Mind, Beginners Mind,* and my interest in Buddhism eventually led me to move to the UK where I worked for several

years within the FWBO. My study of bodhicitta has now led me to other forms of practice; these days I'm wary of shadows of superiority that can linger around the idea of 'me' practising compassion towards 'you'. I'm interested in being present with other people and being patient together with whatever arises. This all has led me to start training as a psychotherapist.

Jarvis Jay Masters

Jarvis Jay Masters arrived in San Quentin in 1981 aged 19, convicted of armed robbery. In 1985, a prison officer was stabbed to death on the second tier of a cell block while Jarvis was locked in his cell. One man was accused of stabbing the sergeant, another was accused of ordering the killing, and Jarvis was accused of sharpening the piece of metal with which he was stabbed. Despite another prisoner's testimony that he, not Jarvis, was the third member of the conspiracy, the trial judge sentenced Jarvis to death. He has been on Death Row since 1990, pending appeals to the California Supreme Court. Jarvis wrote an acclaimed book, *Finding Freedom*, including stories of his life on San Quentin's Death Row and an account of how he became a Buddhist. He is writing a second book, including a memoir of his childhood and youth, as well as more stories of life in San Quentin.

Nissoka

I grew up in the beauty of Devon in south-west England, enjoying being close to the beaches and to Dartmoor. The great expanse and solitude of the moor informed my character and thoughts. At 16 I joined the Parachute Regiment of the British Army and stayed there for five years, serving in Ireland, Kenya, and Botswana. For the next couple of years I lived in my Volkswagen camper by the sea and then moved into my first Buddhist community at the age of 23. Now that I have been ordained and have a daughter, my life has come full circle as I am back in Devon. I take annual trips to India to establish the Bodh Gaya Buddhist Centre and I run meditation and Buddhist classes in Plymouth.

Shubhavajri

As a young woman in the UK Shubhavajri spent many hours in the college library exploring different religions, and learned Transcendental Meditation. That was a support to her through several shocks in her life. A boyfriend died in a motorbike accident, and the spiritual search prompted by her grief led her to Buddhism. She married a member of the Western Buddhist Order and settled with him in New Zealand, and shortly afterwards her brother died suddenly of a brain abscess. In Auckland she started Greens Organics and Café, but in 1997 she was diagnosed with bowel cancer. She filmed an interview with Nagabodhi

187

shortly after her ordination and before her death in June 1998 at the
Auckland Hospice. She took her illness and impending death as an
opportunity to practise her beliefs and share them with others. She was
cremated in the open air, watched by her Buddhist friends.

Subhadramati

I learned to meditate nearly twenty years ago, and, soon after that,
joined my first Buddhist business, a vegetarian restaurant. My initial
motivation was twofold. I wanted to 'give something back' in gratitude
for all that the Buddhist community had given me: encouragement,
support, and a vision for how I could live my life. And I wanted to be
part of a group that was having a positive effect on society at large: to be
living proof that a business could be run in accordance with the principles of generosity and honesty *and* be successful in the marketplace.
At the moment I am having a gap year, in which I am not involved with
any single project, but I could easily see myself working within a
Buddhist team again. Every time I have thought that I have learned
everything there possibly could be to learn from this way of practising, I
have been quickly proved wrong!

Suryagupta

Although I was born in London, I spent my early years in the Carib-
bean. I returned to the East End of London aged 5, and the grimness of
my environment propelled me to search for beauty and a more meaningful name. At the age of 11 I added truth to my quest and encountered
the Dharma while studying law at Bristol University. I immediately
connected with the Buddha, with Sangharakshita, and with his teacher,
Dhardo Rimpoche. Upon ordination in 1997 I was given my name,
which means 'she who is protected or guarded by the sun' (the sun
being an epithet of the Buddha). My search for beauty and truth continues and, via law and social work, I have arrived at story-telling as a
vehicle to enrich, motivate, and inspire others. I now perform and lead
story-telling events across London for people of all ages.

Suvarnaprabha (Suvanna Cullen)

Having grown up in Orange County, which used to be a backwater
suburb of L.A. but recently became groovy, I moved to northern California in 1988. A few years later, while travelling alone in Asia, I was inex-
plicably drawn toward things Buddhist: art, monasticism, meditation.
Many years hence, I am now Director of the small but friendly San Francisco Buddhist Center, leading a relatively unstructured life in which I
sleep too much but occasionally have excellent lucid dreams, keep the
Buddhist Center going, meditate, lead retreats and classes, play guitar,
walk, teach at the jail, read, laugh, write, and occasionally get

depressed. I recently finished my MA in creative writing/poetry, I have directed and performed in Buddhist arts festivals, and I also had a wonderful stint as Buddhist advice columnist Auntie Suvanna in *Dharma Life* magazine. Since March 2006, I have been happily married to person who bears an uncanny resemblance to the obscure but powerful action hero, Left Brain Man.

Vajrasara

I grew up in rural Scotland and graduated in English from Manchester College, Oxford. For ten years I worked as a feature writer and subeditor on national UK newspapers and magazines, and during that time I spent six months living in Spain to write a travel book about Barcelona. I left journalism to spend five years cooking and serving as part of a Buddhist women's team that cooperatively managed a restaurant for the London Buddhist Centre. Then I became director of the FWBO's Communications Office, handling media and interfaith matters for five years. I also helped to edit and produce *Dharma Life* magazine throughout its nine-year life. I currently teach meditation and Buddhism and work as a trainer in nonviolent communication – a process which helps to resolve inner and outer conflict and encourages social change. I have a passion for nature and in my free time enjoy walking, bird-watching, singing, and ruminating.

Vajrashraddha

I was born in London in 1961 and I have two beautiful grown-up children. I now live with my partner in the medieval market town of Faversham in Kent. I work as an auxiliary nurse at a hospice in South London, and before that I had worked in a funeral parlour, the Croydon Buddhist Centre, and a mental health charity. My vision is to see a combined hospice and funeral parlour run according to Buddhist principles. Since writing the article included in this book, I have continued to get fulfilment from working with and supporting people who are confronting the challenge of terminal illness and the last stage of life. I would like to dedicate my article to my inspirational mother, Mary Waugh.

Vidyamala

Originally from New Zealand, I have lived in the UK since 1990, when I moved to Shropshire to live and work at Taraloka Buddhist Retreat Centre for Women. I was ordained within the WBO in 1995 and now live in Manchester. Since 2001 I have been running courses teaching mindfulness-based pain management to anyone wanting to alleviate the suffering associated with chronic pain and ill health. I draw on my own experience of living with chronic pain for thirty years, following a spinal injury I suffered in 1976. In 2004, with two colleagues who are experienced meditators, I formed a company called Breathworks to develop this work. We offer a training programme for others wanting to teach our approach as well as conducting research and training health professionals in the clinical applications of mindfulness. Although I am physically limited by my disability, I am excited by this convergence of the Dharma and the needs of modern health care.

Vishvapani
I became a Buddhist when I was 14, and ever since then I have been exploring what its teachings can mean for me personally and for the society I live in. I founded *Dharma Life* magazine in 1996, when I was based in London and working with the UK national media in their coverage of Buddhism, as well as writing and broadcasting on Buddhism myself. The magazine explored how Buddhism is coming to the West and what it has to offer people in western society. Another strand has been working within the Friends of the Western Buddhist Order, and for three years, up to 2005, I was part of a small group that re-envisioned its structures, especially in the UK. I am currently based in Cardiff, teaching mindfulness, meditation, and Buddhism and working as a freelance writer and broadcaster, still exploring the same themes that have fascinated me over the years.

Brad Warner
After high school, I joined punk band Zero Defex, who soon broke up, leaving a single eighteen-second burst of noise, called *Drop the A-bomb on Me*. In 1993, I went to Japan and realized my childhood dream of helping make low budget man-in-a-rubber-dinosaur-costume monster movies. In the early eighties I became involved in Zen Buddhism, whose no-bullshit philosophy reminded me of punk, and I studied with an iconoclastic Soto Zen Master, Gudo Nishijima, who made me his successor. Disgusted by most of the Buddhist books in bookstores, I published a website called 'Sit Down and Shut Up' and then collated my writings in a book called *Hardcore Zen: Punk Rock, Monster Movies and the Truth About Reality*. After eleven years in Japan, I moved to Los Angeles where I live with my wife Yuka in an apartment filled with Japanese monster memorabilia and pawnshop guitars.

following up

Many more articles from *Dharma Life* are available online at www.dharmalife.com. The Friends of the Western Buddhist Order, the community from which many of these stories grew, has over eighty centres around the world, and you can find out more about it at www.fwbo.org.

There are many excellent books on meditation, Buddhism, and using Buddhist practice to transform the mind in the face of difficulties, so here are a few suggestions of books published by Windhorse Publications. *Change Your Mind* by Paramananda is an inspiring guide to starting to meditate, and Bodhipaksa's *Wildmind* offers systematic instructions. In *Living with Awareness* and *Living with Kindness* Sangharakshita uses traditional Buddhist texts as the springboard for offering guidance on how to apply those teachings in daily life. His book *A Guide to the Buddhist Path* is a good place to start in exploring Buddhist teachings.

For those who want to follow up the work of other contributors, here are some pointers to finding further resources in print and online.

Marian Partington has written a longer account of her journey, entitled 'A Shining Silence', which is online at http://westernchanfellowship.org. She is also a contributor to The Forgiveness Project, which promotes the value of forgiveness: www.theforgivenessproject.com

Jarvis Jay Masters' first book, *Finding Freedom: Writings from Death Row*, is available from Padma Publishing. The campaign to support Jarvis Masters' appeal against his death sentence for murder is online at www.freejarvis.org

Truth and Beauty: A Conversation about Death, the filmed interview with Shubhavajri from which the text of her article is taken, is available on vhs or dvd by emailing Nagabodhi at naga@nagabodhi.com

There is background to the Bearing Witness retreats at Auschwitz in Bernie Glassman's book, *Bearing Witness: A Zen Master's Lessons in Making Peace*, and online at www.zenpeacemakers.org

Transforming our Terror: a spiritual approach to making sense of senseless tragedy by Christopher Titmuss is published by Godsfield Press. His website is www.insightmeditation.org

Living with the Devil: A Meditation on Good and Evil, by Stephen Batchelor, is published by Riverhead Books. His website is www.stephenbatchelor.org

Jan Willis's autobiography, *Dreaming Me: From Baptist to Buddhist, One Woman's Spiritual Journey*, is published by Riverhead Books.

Joan Halifax's books include *The Fruitful Darkness: A Journey Through Buddhist Practice and Tribal Wisdom*, published by HarperCollins.

glossary

Anāpānasali Sutta A Buddhist scripture in which the Buddha teaches an extended version of the mindfulness of breathing meditation practice.

Bardo Literally, 'in-between state', in the Tibetan tradition usually indicating the stage between death and subsequent rebirth.

Bodhisattva A being pledged to gain Enlightenment, though not yet fully Enlightened. The bodhisattva is motivated by compassion and their own wish for Enlightenment grows from the desire to enable others to do the same.

Buddha-nature The teaching found in some Mahāyāna schools that all beings have the potential to gain Enlightenment. Buddha-nature has sometimes been seen as a pure essence at the heart of human experience in which the qualities of Enlightenment are already present.

Dāna Giving or generosity, a key Buddhist practice.

Dharmu The teachings of Buddhism, and also the true nature of reality to which they point.

Green Tāra An 'archetypal' bodhisattva figure, especially popular among Tibetan Buddhists. She is a 'protectoress' and the embodiment of compassion.

Heart Sūtra A short but very important scripture from the Mahāyāna tradition of Buddhism, which is expounds the notion of 'emptiness'.

Karmic The result of karma, or the moral effects of past actions.

Kesa The Zen term for the cloak or robe worn by Buddhist monks and priests. It also refers to a shortened version of the robe that is worn as a shawl, or an even shorter form, which is a band hanging from the neck.

Kleśas The 'poisons' or motivations that drive ordinary human life, keeping it in a cycle that repeatedly leads to suffering. The three principal poisons are greed, hatred, and ignorance.

Mahāyāna Mahāyāna means the 'great way', and refers to a movement within Buddhism, including those Buddhist traditions that emerged later in Buddhist history than the earliest schools, and emphasized the ideal of the bodhisattva.

Mantra A string of sound syllables recited to concentrate the mind. Many Buddhas and bodhisattvas have mantras associated with them.

Mettā bhāvanā A meditation practice aimed at the cultivation of *mettā* or loving-kindness.

Milarepa A saint-like figure from early Tibetan Buddhism who meditated intensively in caves and composed spontaneous verses of teaching and inspiration.

Nine Contemplations of Atīśa A series of esoteric or secret meditation practices performed within certain tantric traditions of Tibetan Buddhism and aimed at cultivating special mental powers, some of which are particularly relevant at the time of death.

Phowa The Tibetan Buddhist practice of guiding the direction taken by one's consciousness at the time of death towards a more fortunate rebirth.

Pratītya-samutpāda 'Dependent arising'. The Buddha's fundamental teaching on the nature of reality which states that all things come into being and cease to exist in dependence upon conditions.

Prostration A full-length bow, which involves lying face-down with the whole of one's body flat on the floor.

Refuges Those things on which Buddhist tradition teaches it is wise to rely. The three Refuges for Buddhists are the Buddha – the historical teacher who gained Enlightenment and the ideal of Enlightenment that is open to all; the Dharma – the teachings of Buddhism and the truth they contain; and the Sangha – the community of all those who have gained Enlightenment.

Rimpoche A 'precious teacher' in Tibetan Buddhism. The term is usually applied to people considered to be the rebirth of a previous master.

Roshi A 'venerable master' in the Zen Buddhist tradition.

Saṃsāra The cyclic round of rebirth, characterized by suffering, which can only be ended by the attainment of Enlightenment.

Sangha The community of practitioners of Buddhism, and all those who have gained Enlightenment.

Śākyamuni Buddha The 'sage of the Śākyans', an alternative name for Gautama Buddha, the historical Buddha.

Śūnyatā 'Emptiness' or 'voidness'. The Mahāyāna teaching that nothing has a fixed or permanent essence.

Sutta (Pali) or *sūtra (Sanskrit)* A scripture or text recounting a discourse or teaching of the Buddha.

Take refuge The act of commitment to the Three Refuges through which one becomes a Buddhist and later reaffirms that commitment.

Team-based right livelihood The practice within the Friends of the Western Buddhist Order of Buddhists working together.

Theravādin Belonging to the Theravāda school, 'the school of the elders', which is prevalent in Burma, Thailand, Cambodia, Laos, and Sri Lanka.

Tibetan Wheel of Becoming or *Wheel of Life* A visual representation of Buddhist teachings in a painting showing the process through which greed, hatred, and ignorance lead to rebirth in various realms of existence.

Tonglen The Tibetan Buddhist practice aimed at developing compassion, of sending out one's own happiness and good fortune, and receiving others' suffering and negativity.

Vajrasattva A Buddha or bodhisattva figure connected with purity. He is depicted as white in colour and holding a diamond-thunderbolt in his right hand.

Vinaya The code of conduct that governs the behaviour of Buddhist monks and nuns.

Vipassanā 'Insight' or 'understanding'. Some meditation practices are termed 'vipassanā' because their main aim is the attainment of insight, rather than concentration and calm. In the West, some of the best-known meditation teachers teach vipassanā in the Insight Meditation Movement.

Zazen The open, reflective Zen meditation practice.

Zendo A Zen meditation hall.

The windhorse symbolizes the energy of the Enlightened mind carrying the truth of the Buddha's teachings to all corners of the world. On its back the windhorse bears three jewels: a brilliant gold jewel represents the Buddha, the ideal of Enlightenment, a sparkling blue jewel represents the teachings of the Buddha, the Dharma, and a glowing red jewel, the community of the Buddha's enlightened followers, the Sangha. Windhorse Publications, through the medium of books, similarly takes these three jewels out to the world.

Windhorse Publications is a Buddhist publishing house, staffed by practising Buddhists. We place great emphasis on producing books of high quality, accessible and relevant to those interested in Buddhism at whatever level. Drawing on the whole range of the Buddhist tradition, our books include translations of traditional texts, commentaries, books that make links with Western culture and ways of life, biographies of Buddhists, and works on meditation.

As a charitable institution we welcome donations to help us continue our work. We also welcome manuscripts on aspects of Buddhism or meditation. For orders and catalogues log on to www.windhorsepublications.com or contact:

Windhorse Publications	Consortium	Windhorse Books
11 Park Road	1045 Westgate Drive	PO Box 574
Birmingham	St Paul MN 55114	Newtown NSW 2042
B13 8AB	USA	Australia
UK		

Windhorse Publications is an arm of the Friends of the Western Buddhist Order, which has more than sixty centres on four continents. Through these centres, members of the Western Buddhist Order offer regular programmes of events for the general public and for more experienced students. These include meditation classes, public talks, study on Buddhist themes and texts, and bodywork classes such as t'ai chi, yoga, and massage. The FWBO also runs several retreat centres and the Karuna Trust, a fundraising charity that supports social welfare projects in the slums and villages of India.

Many FWBO centres have residential spiritual communities and ethical businesses associated with them. Arts activities are encouraged too, as is the development of strong bonds of friendship between people who share the same ideals. In this way the FWBO is developing a unique approach to Buddhism, not simply as a set of techniques, but as a creatively directed way of life for people living in the modern world.

If you would like more information about the FWBO please visit the website at www.fwbo.org or write to:

London Buddhist Centre	Aryaloka	Sydney Buddhist Centre
51 Roman Road	14 Heartwood Circle	24 Enmore Road
London	Newmarket NH 03857	Newtown NSW 2042
E2 0HU	USA	Australia
UK		

ALSO FROM WINDHORSE PUBLICATIONS

A Guide to the Buddhist Path
by Sangharakshita

Which Buddhist teachings really matter? How does one begin to practise them in a systematic way? Without a guide one can easily get dispirited or lost.

In this highly readable anthology a leading Western Buddhist sorts out fact from myth, essence from cultural accident, to reveal the fundamental ideals and teachings of Buddhism. The result is a reliable map of the Buddhist path that anyone can follow.

Sangharakshita is an ideal companion on the path. As founder of a major Western Buddhist movement he has helped thousands of people to make an effective contact with the richness and beauty of the Buddha's teachings.

240 pages, with black-and-white illustrations
ISBN 1 899579 04 4
£14.99/$24.95

The Breath

by Vessantara

The breath: always with us, necessary to our very existence, but often unnoticed. Yet giving it attention can transform our lives.

This is a very useful combination of practical instruction on the mindfulness of breathing with much broader lessons on where the breath can lead us. Vessantara, a meditator of many years experience, offers us:

> * Clear instruction on how to meditate on the breath
> * Practical ways to integrate meditation into our lives
> * Suggestions for deepening calm and concentration
> * Advice on how to let go and dive into experience
> * Insights into the lessons of the breath

The Breath returns us again and again to the fundamental and precious experience of being alive.

144 pages
ISBN 1 899579 69 9
£6.99/$10.95/€10.95

The **art of meditation** series continues with *The Heart*, available in late 2006.

WHAT BUDDHISM CAN OFFER

To survive the twenty-first century we need to develop new ways of responding to each other and the planet, discover new paths to wisdom, combined with a growing sense of awareness of the consequences of our actions.

A new series from Windhorse Publications seeks to explore the fruits of western exploration of Buddhism to see what practical contribution it can make to our lives. In the books in this series we discover how Buddhist practices and teachings can help us live life more fully in the twenty-first century – whether we are Buddhist or not.

Suitable for people of any faith – or no faith – each book looks at a universal life issue and offers tools for change and growth. Drawing on the experiences of a variety of people, these books share what works, and how, in an engaging and practical way.

The series covers topics as diverse as

> * Parenting
> * Communication
> * Working with physical pain
> * Ageing
> * Coping with stress and anxiety